Cyber Mission Thread Analysis

An Implementation Guide for Process Planning and Execution

LAUREN A. MAYER, DON SNYDER, GUY WEICHENBERG,
DANIELLE C. TARRAF, JONATHAN W. WELBURN, SUZANNE GENC,
MYRON HURA, BERNARD FOX

Prepared for the Department of the Air Force
Approved for public release; distribution unlimited

RAND PROJECT AIR FORCE

For more information on this publication, visit **www.rand.org/t/RR3188z2**.

About RAND

The RAND Corporation is a research organization that develops solutions to public policy challenges to help make communities throughout the world safer and more secure, healthier and more prosperous. RAND is nonprofit, nonpartisan, and committed to the public interest. To learn more about RAND, visit www.rand.org.

Research Integrity

Our mission to help improve policy and decisionmaking through research and analysis is enabled through our core values of quality and objectivity and our unwavering commitment to the highest level of integrity and ethical behavior. To help ensure our research and analysis are rigorous, objective, and nonpartisan, we subject our research publications to a robust and exacting quality-assurance process; avoid both the appearance and reality of financial and other conflicts of interest through staff training, project screening, and a policy of mandatory disclosure; and pursue transparency in our research engagements through our commitment to the open publication of our research findings and recommendations, disclosure of the source of funding of published research, and policies to ensure intellectual independence. For more information, visit www.rand.org/about/principles.

RAND's publications do not necessarily reflect the opinions of its research clients and sponsors.

Published by the RAND Corporation, Santa Monica, Calif.
© 2022 RAND Corporation
RAND® is a registered trademark.

Library of Congress Cataloging-in-Publication Data is available for this publication.

ISBN: 978-1-9774-0808-2

Cover: *Master Sgt. Mike R. Smith/U.S. Air National Guard.*

Preface

This report presents a guide for implementing the cyber mission thread analysis (CMTA) process for assessing the cybersecurity risk of weapon systems incorporating mission impact. Both are results of a project jointly sponsored by Jeffrey Stanley, Assistant Secretary of the Air Force for Science, Technology, and Engineering, Office of the Assistant Secretary of the Air Force for Acquisition and Logistics; and Dennis Miller, Director of Engineering and Technical Management, Air Force Life Cycle Management Center. The CMTA process was previously developed by RAND Project AIR FORCE (RAND PAF) in fiscal year (FY) 2015 and subsequently revised based on a pilot application in FY 2016. The guide presented in the document draws on best practices from relevant literature and lessons learned during the iterative refinement of the process.

This report is a companion to our CMTA methodology report (Snyder et al., 2022), which the reader is presumed to have read and which describes a framework for prioritizing systems for further analysis. The details of implementation—that is, who should do CMTA, when and where it should take place, and how to accomplish it—are also important for a successful outcome and are described in this report. Since the implementation of CMTA relies heavily on engagement with subject-matter experts (SMEs) through interviews or focus groups, this report summarizes relevant guidance from the social and decision sciences literature and applies such guidance to suggest a number of implementation strategies that can be employed specifically during the CMTA process. The report additionally provides lessons learned during implementation of CMTA during a pilot on the aerial refueling mission as part of the Line of Action #1 of the U.S. Air Force Cyber Campaign Plan.

The report has two primary intended audiences: the individuals in the organization(s) that would own the CMTA process, and those organizations and teams that would be responsible for carrying out the CMTA for a mission area. The first audience would be responsible for selecting the organization to carry out the process for different mission areas, and this report suggests attributes and selection criteria for doing so. The second audience would be responsible for the detailed planning and execution of the CMTA process for a mission area, and this report provides guidance on how to carry out these responsibilities. Beyond these two specific audiences, this report may be of interest to the broader cybersecurity, acquisition, and operational communities. Finally, many of the recommendations and discussions should be helpful for individuals who are developing other analytic processes conducted by teams, in which subject-matter expertise is a main component, such as the high-performance teams (HPTs) developing Joint Capabilities Integration and Development System (JCIDS)[1] requirements documents.

The research reported here was conducted within the Resource Management Program of RAND Project AIR FORCE.

RAND Project AIR FORCE

RAND Project AIR FORCE (PAF), a division of the RAND Corporation, is the Department of the Air Force's (DAF's) federally funded research and development center for studies and analyses, supporting both the United States Air Force and the United States Space Force. PAF provides the DAF with independent analyses of policy alternatives affecting the development, employment, combat readiness, and support of current and future air, space, and cyber forces. Research is conducted in four programs: Strategy and Doctrine; Force Modernization and Employment; Resource Management; and Workforce, Development, and Health. The research reported here was prepared under contract FA7014-16-D-1000.

Additional information about PAF is available on our website: www.rand.org/paf/

This report documents work originally shared with the U.S. Air Force on May 30, 2018. The draft report, issued on September 28, 2017, was reviewed by formal peer reviewers and U.S. Air Force SMEs.

---

[1] JCIDS is one of three major Department of Defense (DoD) processes that support delivery of capabilities to the warfighter. It supports the Chairman of the Joint Chiefs of Staff and the Joint Requirements Oversight Council in identifying and assessing capability needs of the warfighter through a collaborative process. If an acquisition program is started, it is based on the identification of capability needs through JCIDS. See Chairman of the Joint Chiefs of Staff, Instruction 3170.01, for further information.

Contents

Preface iii

Figures vi

Tables vii

Summary.. viii

Acknowledgments xii

Abbreviations xiii

1. Overview of the CMTA Implementation Guide 1

    Introduction 1

    Overview of the Process... 3

    Timeline and Strategies for Efficiencies 6

    Organization of the Report 6

2. Phase One: Establishing CMTA Roles and Analysis Inputs..................................... 8

    Selecting an Executing Organization 9

    Assembling the Analyst Team.. 9

    Gathering and Reviewing Relevant Documents.. 11

    Identifying and Recruiting SMEs.. 12

3. Phase Two: Planning the Analysis Process 15

    Developing the Analysis Plan 15

    Planning Logistics and Preparing Materials.. 22

4. Phase Three: Conducting the Analysis.. 23

    Developing the Initial Mission Thread... 24

    Reviewing the Initial Mission Thread 26

    Ranking Systems 29

    Reviewing CMTA Results 30

    Time-Saving Variations... 31

    Performing Post-Analysis Activities 32

5. Adopting CMTA Process Efficiencies 33

    Documenting, Collecting, and Leveraging Lessons Learned.................................... 33

    Developing Mission Thread Templates.. 34

    Designating Dedicated Analyst Teams or an Analyst Team Trainer 34

    Managing the Concurrency of CMTAs... 35

    Managing the Order of CMTAs 36

6. Final Thoughts and Next Steps.. 37

Appendix A. Further Considerations for Conducting SME Elicitations.......................... 39

Appendix B. CMTA Analyst Team Checklist 49

References 54

Figures

Figure S.1. Overview of the CMTA Process with Stakeholder Responsibilities............................x

Figure 1.1. Overview of the CMTA Process with Stakeholder Responsibilities............................3

Figure 4.1. A Proposed Analysis Plan and Timeline for Phase Three (Conducting the Analysis)..23

Figure 4.2. Generic Format of a Functional Flow Block Diagram 26

Tables

Table 3.1. Advantages and Limitations of the SME Engagement Types......................................17
Table 5.1. A Visualization of Concurrent CMTA Processes for Three Missions.........................35

Summary

In FY 2016, the U.S. Air Force began implementing a process for identifying mission-critical systems in a cyber threat environment. This process, called cyber mission thread analysis (CMTA), is based on a methodology developed by RAND Project AIR FORCE and continues to evolve (Snyder et al., 2022). CMTA is a top-down approach for ranking systems according to their potential *mission impact* given a cyber attack. The idea of CMTA is to reduce the number of systems requiring a detailed *vulnerability* and *threat* analysis by triaging systems based on mission impact.[1]

There is a need to do such an analysis broadly across all the missions in the U.S. Air Force. The number of missions to assess is estimated to be more than 40 (Miller, Scarano, and Tashji, 2017). Given this large number, coupled with the reality that mission impact is just the first step (to be followed by selective assessments of vulnerability and threat), the CMTA process must not take more than a few months for each mission if it is to be of value.

Early experience with the CMTA indicates a need for a disciplined, well-planned process for executing each CMTA in order to do CMTA expeditiously while still giving results good enough to make decisions about mission criticality. Additionally, to exhaustively analyze all U.S. Air Force missions, some number of CMTAs will need to be performed concurrently rather than sequentially. This report provides a proposed guide for the planning and implementation of CMTA to reach these ends. Nevertheless, we expect that, with lessons learned upon executing future CMTAs, the ideas presented in this report will be further refined.

In this implementation guide, we detail the roles and responsibilities of organizations and personnel involved in CMTA; the process for implementing such an analysis and the types of preparations necessary for successful implementation; a rough timeline required to perform CMTA for one or more missions concurrently; and the possible constraints and issues that may be encountered. The implementation guide acts as a companion document to Snyder et al. (2022), which describes the analytical tasks that must be carried out to perform CMTA. It assumes the reader has read this document or is otherwise familiar with the CMTA framework. Although targeted at CMTA, many of the principles we outline in this report will be useful for planning similar analysis activities.

---

[1] For unfamiliar readers, this approach begins by defining and scoping a mission that is then decomposed into mission elements and the functional flow between those elements. Next, systems are identified that support each of the elements. This method produces a "mission thread," which is then analyzed to determine the relative mission impact of cyber attacks, or "criticality," of the mission elements and/or systems. System criticality is assessed using a number of system attributes that can be computed directly from the mission thread. The analysis produces a relative ranking of systems that can be used to triage which systems are assigned for further vulnerability and threat assessments.

CMTA Roles

To effectively execute the CMTA process, we define the following stakeholder roles:

- **CMTA process owner:** The CMTA process owner owns and defines the methodology for CMTA. It manages the overall process for assessing all missions and provides resources to support CMTA exercises. The CMTA process owner selects each organization that will implement CMTA at the mission level, orchestrates the overall timing of CMTA exercises, and gathers lessons learned from each CMTA exercise to institutionalize them for future exercises. The CMTA process owner also plays a key role in securing the availability and buy-in of subject-matter experts (SMEs), who provide necessary expertise for the analysis.
- **Executing organization:** The executing organization, assigned by the CMTA process owner, manages the CMTA process for a specific mission. It is in charge of assembling the analyst team to perform the CMTA.
- **Analyst team:** The analyst team plans and performs the CMTA. Collectively, the team requires knowledge of the CMTA process and the mission being analyzed. The more knowledge the team has of the relevant systems supporting that mission, the more efficient and effective it can be. Team member roles include a team leader, a specific individual to interview and/or facilitate group discussions with experts, an individual to perform process mapping (i.e., to build the functional flow block diagram of the mission thread in appropriate software), and a note-taker.
- **Subject-matter experts:** Individuals with mission- and system-level expertise provide the analyst team with information to support their analyses. SMEs are needed from two main areas of expertise: system-independent activities that take place during the operation of the mission, and technical and engineering knowledge of all the systems used during mission operations.

CMTA Implementation

We describe three phases of CMTA implementation: (1) establish roles and analytic inputs, (2) plan the analysis process, and (3) conduct the analysis. These phases are shown graphically along with the activities of the key stakeholders in Figure S.1.

- **Establish roles and analytic inputs:** In this first phase, the CMTA process owner defines the mission and scope of the mission for a CMTA. The execution of this CMTA is assigned to an executing organization, SMEs are identified, and relevant artifacts such as existing architectures and concepts of operations (CONOPS) are collected.
- **Plan the analysis process:** In this second phase, an overall plan is established for conducting the analysis, including scheduling meetings with SMEs, both internal and external to the executing organization. Protocols for SME engagements are written and logistics are managed.
- **Conduct the analysis:** In this third phase, the bulk of the CMTA work is performed. The main activities are to build a mission thread, review the mission thread for accuracy, rank the systems by criticality to mission, and review and report final results. In all, we estimate that implementing the analysis could have a targeted timeline of six weeks using

this proposed analysis plan. If the number of SMEs is large or scheduling issues emerge, the timing may increase. To perform this analysis most efficiently, we propose implementation in four steps:

1. The analyst team builds a draft of the mission thread based on artifacts collected, SME interviews, and analyst team knowledge of the mission area and supporting systems.
2. The analyst team subjects the mission thread to a review by external SMEs during direct, face-to-face engagements to revise and complete a final mission thread. The goal of this step is to get the SMEs to agree that the mission thread content accurately matches what they expressed during the initial interviews. This vetting process is critical to instill confidence in the final CMTA.
3. The analyst team next uses the mission thread to rank the criticality of systems to the mission, as outlined in Snyder et al. (2022).
4. Finally, the analyst team compiles the findings and sends them to the SMEs for comment. If the CMTA methodology does not identify a system that SMEs deem to be critical, the mission thread may need further revising. However, if the mission thread is correct, then instead, the CMTA methodology itself may need revising. The latter feedback will improve the process.

Figure S.1. Overview of the CMTA Process with Stakeholder Responsibilities

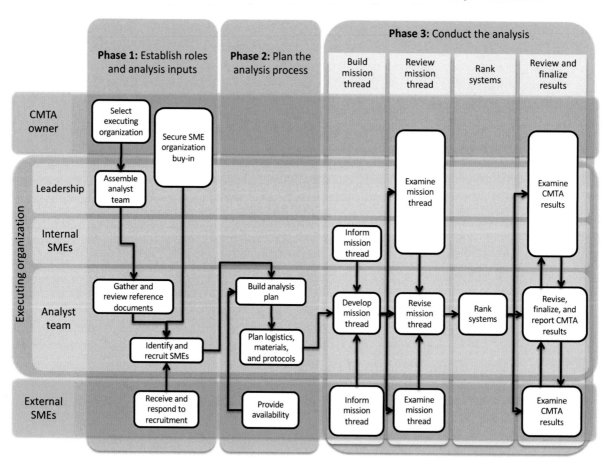

NOTES: Arrows in figure represent dependencies; CMTA process timeline reads from left to right.

Considerations when Planning and Executing the CMTA Process

As more CMTAs are performed, teams will climb a learning curve, resulting in the process running more smoothly and quickly. We estimate that initial CMTAs may require two or more months to plan and an additional two months to execute. As experience is gained, however, a CMTA for one mission could be targeted for completion in less than two months. These time estimates presume that tools for collecting data, depicting a mission thread, and analyzing for criticality already exist.

We highlight here a few considerations to keep in mind when performing the process. The first two points are likely the most critical to efficiently and effectively implementing the CMTA process, but all points below should be considered if the effort is to be truly a success.

- *Planning is crucial.* To efficiently and effectively implement the CMTA process, the analyst team should develop and execute a detailed plan. The number of stakeholders involved and the desire for a swift timeline require a substantial coordination effort.
- *Remember the ultimate goal of CMTA.* Throughout the entire analysis, the analyst team should remember the ultimate CMTA goal—producing a list of systems for further cyber assessments. The purpose is triage: It is vital that any mission-critical system appear highly ranked; it is okay if some noncritical systems appear highly ranked. This goal ensures that SME and analyst discussions do not become unnecessarily detailed and CMTA results remain within scope.
- *Tailoring the process is necessary.* There is no one-size-fits-all model for implementing CMTA. The process will differ based on the complexity of the mission being analyzed, the classification level, the desired timeline, the available resources, and the level of expertise and availability of involved personnel. Therefore, while this implementation guide provides commonsense recommendations on how to plan and execute CMTA under most circumstances, every CMTA exercise will require some degree of tailoring to successfully execute.
- *Periodic critical reviews on CMTA results by all CMTA stakeholders are important.* The CMTA exercise should be seen as a collaborative effort. The analyst team should both incorporate inputs from CMTA stakeholders and, importantly, elicit their feedback on the analytic products. Critical review should help to ensure CMTA results are accurate, foster stakeholder buy-in, and instill credibility in the process. Ultimately, decisionmakers will have confidence in the results if the personnel involved are the best available and the process is transparent and reasonable.
- *Incorporate learning from prior CMTAs.* As more CMTAs are performed, the CMTA process owner should develop a repository for lessons learned, sample CMTA materials (e.g., SME questionnaires), and mission thread templates. Analyst teams can make heavy use of such documents throughout the CMTA process.
- *CMTAs for multiple missions will likely need to be coordinated.* Given the number of missions needing analysis, a serial application of CMTAs may lead to a long overall time frame. Many of the CONOPS for missions could change in that time, requiring reanalysis. The CMTA process owner likely needs to assign multiple CMTAs to be performed concurrently. Proper management of this CMTA concurrency (e.g., ordering of missions) is crucial.

Acknowledgments

We thank Jeffrey Stanley and Dennis Miller for sponsoring this work and for supporting its execution. Many others in the U.S. Air Force and at MITRE, too numerous to mention by name, also helped and supported us.

At RAND, we thank Rebecca Balebako, Elizabeth Bodine-Baron, John Drew, Kristin Lynch, Brynn Tannehill, and Laura Werber for helpful discussions and for reviewing earlier versions of this implementation guide; Lionel Galway, Andrew Lauland, and Isaac Porsche for their analytic reviews; and Michelle Horner and Jordan Bresnahan for their administrative assistance.

That we received help and insights from those acknowledged above should not be taken to imply that they concur with the views expressed in this report. We alone are responsible for the content, including any errors or oversights.

Abbreviations

AoA	analysis of alternatives
CMTA	cyber mission thread analysis
CO	commanding officer
CONOPS	concepts of operations
DoD	Department of Defense
DoDAF	Department of Defense Architecture Framework
FY	fiscal year
HPT	high-performance team
JCIDS	Joint Capabilities Integration and Development System
KPP	key performance parameter
LOA	line of action
MAJCOM	major command
OV	operations view
SME	subject-matter expert
SV	systems view
TTP	tactics, techniques, and procedures

1. Overview of the CMTA Implementation Guide

Introduction

As the U.S. Air Force looks to improve the cybersecurity and cyber resiliency of its weapon systems, it must decide how it should concentrate its efforts and finite resources to best manage cybersecurity risks. In fiscal year (FY) 2016, the U.S. Air Force began implementing a process for identifying mission-critical systems in a cyber threat environment. This process, called cyber mission thread analysis (CMTA), is based on a methodology developed by RAND Project AIR FORCE and continues to evolve. The development and institutionalization of CMTA is one of seven lines of action (LOAs) in the U.S. Air Force Cyber Campaign Plan. This LOA includes six objectives, one of which is to develop a common, repeatable methodology for CMTA, which is the focus of Snyder et al. (2022) and this companion report. Other objectives, which are outside the scope of this report, include identifying the mission threads, executing CMTA for the mission threads, and developing analytic tools to implement CMTA.

CMTA is a top-down approach for ranking systems according to their potential *mission impact* given a cyber attack. First, a functional flow of a mission, or mission thread, is developed such that systems used in that mission can be identified at an appropriate level of detail. Systems are then ranked in terms of a number of criteria that represent their criticality to the mission. The idea of CMTA is to reduce the number of systems requiring a detailed *vulnerability* and *threat* analysis by triaging systems based on mission impact. Overall, the intent of the CMTA exercise should not be to generate a perfect mission thread map and reach consensus on the relative importance of every system; rather, it should be a solution that inspires confidence that the *critical* elements have been identified in order to provide a sound basis for decisionmaking.

There is a need to do such an analysis broadly across all the missions in the U.S. Air Force. The number of missions to assess is estimated to be more than 40 (Miller, Scarano, and Tashji, 2017). Given the number of missions to assess for criticality of systems to mission impact, coupled with the reality that mission impact is just the first step (to be followed by selective assessments of vulnerability and threat), the CMTA process must not take more than a few months for each mission if the process is to be of value.

Early experience with the CMTA indicates a need for a disciplined, well-planned process for executing each CMTA in order to do it expeditiously while still giving results good enough to make decisions about mission criticality. While Snyder et al. (2022) describes what analytical tasks must be carried out to perform the CMTA, the purpose of this report is to guide the implementation of those tasks. At a high level, there are three main tasks that need to be done: (1) define the scope of a mission to be assessed for the CMTA and assign it to some organization to execute; (2) produce a "thread" (map) of that mission that captures all key mission elements and systems that support the execution of those mission elements, and critically review its accuracy; and (3) perform a criticality analysis of the thread to list the systems most likely to be critical to the mission.

In this implementation guide, we propose roles and responsibilities of organizations and personnel to conduct these three tasks; the process for implementing them and the types of preparations necessary for successful implementation; a rough timeline required to perform CMTA for one or more missions concurrently; and the possible constraints and issues that may be encountered. As we will describe more thoroughly in later chapters, there is no one-size-fits-all model for implementing CMTA. Therefore, we provide a generalized form of a proposed process along with methods to customize it, including the advantages and limitations of such methods for differing situations. We also include guidance on effectively coordinating the analyses of multiple missions.

The process for implementing a CMTA outlined in this report is a proposed set of planned, orchestrated steps. It is based on a survey of best practices in the literature and some experience from an initial CMTA on the aerial refueling mission conducted in FY 2016 by the U.S. Air Force. As further experience is gained, we fully expect that the process of doing CMTAs will improve and some of the details we propose in this report will be superseded. Our intent is that this document might save time and increase the utility of the initial CMTAs that are performed and thereby accelerate the progress up a learning curve.

Given that the CMTA process relies heavily on engagements with subject-matter experts (SMEs), the implementation guide draws from the foundational body of literature related to best practices of a number of social science methods, including methods for conducting interviews and focus groups. Instead of merely citing such literature, which would require readers to obtain and survey it themselves, we synthesize and summarize the literature in this report, and apply it specifically for the application of CMTA. In doing so, we hoped to provide a one-stop resource for CMTA implementation.

When developing the proposed steps in this implementation guide, we kept in mind the ultimate goal of CMTA—to produce results that ultimately can be briefed to high-level officials for decisionmaking. Such a goal requires confidence in the results. To obtain this level of confidence, then, the CMTA process should be transparent, reproducible, and understandable. Analysis should be based on the best information available and involve relevant, credible stakeholders. At the same time, the process should produce results in a timely and efficient manner. The purpose is one of triage—to conservatively capture all critical elements, even at the expense of including some noncritical ones. This treatment should help to ensure the process is not overly laborious.

We present our suggestions using a two-tiered approach. The first tier, in the main body of this report, details the primary actions that CMTA stakeholders can perform to ensure a successful process. The second tier, in Appendix A, provides secondary issues for users of this implementation guide that may be considered once the primary actions have been grasped. In addition to the tiered-approach of this implementation guide, we provide a simplified checklist in Appendix B that maps to the phases of the CMTA process and provides for additional administrative details. As we will discuss in future chapters, every CMTA exercise presents its own set of unique circumstances and therefore requires some degree of tailoring to successfully execute. While the main purpose of this report is to guide the CMTA process, many of the suggestions and discussions should be helpful for individuals who are developing other analytic processes conducted by teams, in which subject-matter expertise is a main component, such as the high-performance teams (HPTs) developing Joint Capabilities Integration and Development System (JCIDS)[1] requirements documents.

Overview of the Process

The process we describe in this document creates a plan for all the CMTA stakeholders, as depicted in Figure 1.1 and described below.

Figure 1.1. Overview of the CMTA Process with Stakeholder Responsibilities

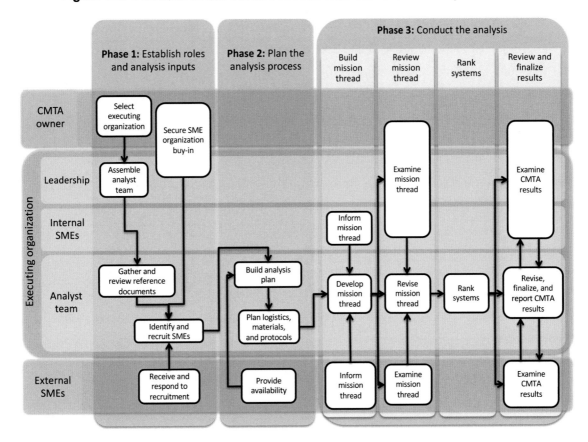

NOTES: Arrows in figure represent dependencies; CMTA process timeline reads from left to right.

---

[1] JCIDS is one of three major DoD processes that support delivery of capabilities to the warfighter. It supports the Chairman of the Joint Chiefs of Staff and the Joint Requirements Oversight Council in identifying and assessing capability needs of the warfighter through a collaborative process. If an acquisition program is started, it is based on the identification of capability needs through JCIDS. See Chairman of the Joint Chiefs of Staff, Instruction 3170.01, for further information.

Phase One. The process begins with the *CMTA process owner*, a single organization that manages the CMTA process for all missions and ensures that sufficient resources (i.e., funding and personnel) are available to conduct the CMTA.[2] For each mission (or set of missions) being analyzed, the CMTA process owner chooses an organization to be the *executing organization* in charge of managing the analysis for that specific mission. Based on the desired timeline for CMTA completion and anticipated resources, the CMTA process owner, in collaboration with the executing organization, should then establish the scope of the CMTA, which can be adjusted as the CMTA progresses. The executing organization next assembles an *analyst team* from within or outside its organization to perform the analysis. Members of the analyst team should have previous knowledge of the mission area and be trained (or trainable) in the CMTA process. At least one member of this team should be trained (or trainable) in process mapping (to build the functional flow block diagram of the mission thread using available software) and in interviewing and/or group facilitation. The latter role is an important one as the analyst team needs to select and elicit information from appropriate *SMEs* to comprehensively cover areas of specific mission operations and systems expertise not represented within the analyst team. These SMEs may be found both internal to the executing organization (e.g., experienced operators) and externally throughout the U.S. Air Force or at relevant contractors, and they inform every part of the analyst team's analysis, from building the mission thread to identifying systems.

With all of the appropriate personnel and organizational roles assigned and funding secured, the analyst team can begin to gather the relevant operational mission and system reference documents (e.g., operational architectures) and recruit SMEs. Ensuring active engagement from the best external SMEs will likely require buy-in from the leadership of SME organizations, which may require participation from leadership of the CMTA process owner and the executing organization.

Phase Two. The CMTA process also necessitates that the analyst team develop a structured analysis plan to outline how, where, and when CMTA stakeholders will be engaged. This process can, for example, address whether information from SMEs will be elicited using questionnaires, interviews, or focus groups and when CMTA stakeholders will have the opportunity to critically review the analysis. The design of this analysis plan depends on a number of factors, including the complexity of the mission, classification level, the expertise contained within the analyst team and executing organization, the availability and proximity of external SMEs, and the quality and availability of operational mission and system reference documents. With an analysis plan in place, the analyst team should make detailed preparations for the analysis, including logistics planning for the SME engagements, developing materials that SMEs can use before or during any of these engagements, and importantly, developing protocols

---

[2] The CMTA process owner should not be confused with major commands (MAJCOMs), which own the missions.

4

that outline the procedure (e.g., questions to be asked, focus group schedule) to be used during the SME engagements.

Phase Three. Finally, the analyst team can execute the preliminary analysis plan, designed as part of phase two. Using operational mission and system reference documents and SME inputs, the team builds an initial mission thread, including both a functional flow block diagram of the mission and identification of associated systems. The level of external SME involvement at this stage depends on the quality of reference documents, as well as analyst team and internal SME knowledge of the mission and systems. If the analyst team is able to build a majority of the initial mission thread using its own knowledge, with documentation and SME expertise internal to the executing organization, engagements with external SMEs may only involve very specific probes to fill in residual gaps in the thread. However, if major portions of the mission thread are missing, the analyst team may need to interview SMEs using exploratory questions to elicit large sections of or perhaps the entire thread. In either case, this initial SME engagement can likely be completed through phone interviews.

After developing the initial mission thread, the analyst team can conduct a critical review with both internal and external SMEs to ensure that the thread represents mission operations as the SMEs understand them to be. As a part of this step, SMEs will have a chance to see the entire mission thread for the first time and critique it. Additionally, any remaining issues such as mission thread gaps or conflicting information gathered during its development can be presented to SMEs for resolution. These types of activities may be best completed with external SMEs as one or more in-person focus groups and with internal SMEs as an emailed or online questionnaire. Around the same time as the SME critical review, the analyst team also can elicit feedback on the mission thread from the CMTA process owner and the executing organization's leadership to ensure the results are appropriately scoped and meeting the objectives of the CMTA process.

After the first critical review, the analyst team can conduct another iteration on the mission thread. Further analysis of this mission thread will produce a ranking of the systems according to a set of criticality criteria, as described in Snyder et al. (2022), that can direct further vulnerability and threat assessments.

Finally, the analyst team can perform a final critical review—this time on the system rankings and mission thread as necessary. Again, this critical review may involve engaging appropriate internal and external SMEs, as well as the CMTA process owner and executing organization leadership, to allow them to react and recommend any changes to the draft final product. To be respectful of SMEs' time and not exhaust their willingness for involvement, this SME engagement could take place using some combination of emailed or online questionnaires and phone interviews. Afterward, the analyst team may convene to update the mission thread and system rankings based on input received. More than one critical review engagement may be needed to receive feedback from all CMTA stakeholders on the CMTA results. Therefore, this final process step is represented as a two-way arrow in Figure 1.1, indicating the possibility of iterative refinement.

While not represented in the figure, we suggest that the final CMTA results be reexamined periodically for further refinements. The CONOPS of missions and design of systems under which operational mission must be considered all may change in the future. These factors may result in changes to the mission thread that introduce new systems or change the criticality of existing systems. The prioritization of systems for further cybersecurity assessments may therefore be adjusted. Such an activity requires continuous monitoring of changes by the CMTA process owner and may result in a small reanalysis effort by the original or a new executing organization.

Timeline and Strategies for Efficiencies

As with any process, we expect the CMTA procedure to take longer for the first few missions for which it is implemented, but for the timeline to decrease as lessons learned are collected and templates (e.g., for the SME engagement materials and mission threads) are refined. We estimate that the preparatory phases of the process (phases one and two, as depicted in Figure 1.1) may require a couple of months for the first few missions, but then shorten to a couple of weeks as experience with the process builds. We expect that conducting the actual analysis (phase three, as depicted in Figure 1.1) will require approximately six weeks to complete for most missions,[3] and this time too should decrease as efficiencies are realized.

We propose a number of strategies the analyst team can perform to increase efficiency of the CMTA process. The CMTA process owner could provide the analyst team with reference materials that include lessons learned, past CMTA results, mission thread templates, and exemplar SME engagement materials (e.g., questionnaires). The analyst team can leverage all of these to reduce the CMTA process timeline. A further strategy that may reduce the overall CMTA timeline for all missions is to perform analyses on multiple missions concurrently. These concurrent CMTAs can be performed by the same, or more than one, executing organization, but may need to have offset starting times to ensure that the CMTA process owner is available when the phase of the process warrants.

Organization of the Report

The remainder of this report parallels the organization of the implementation of the CMTA process, as depicted by the columns in Figure 1.1. Chapter 2 details the roles of the CMTA stakeholders and how to select appropriate organizations and individuals so that all inputs for the analysis are established. Chapter 3 describes how the analyst team can prepare for the analysis, which results in an analysis plan and logistical plan to implement the third phase of the CMTA process. Chapter 4 then describes a proposed implementation of this analysis plan across four

---

[3] These time estimates presume that tools for collecting data, depicting a mission thread, and analyzing for criticality already exist.

subphases. Chapter 5 discusses strategies to improve the efficiency of the CMTA process and decrease its overall timeline. Chapter 6 concludes this report with some final considerations. We also include two appendixes, one with further details on SME elicitations (details that are applicable well beyond the CMTA application), and a second that has a simple checklist that analyst teams can use when conducting the CMTA process. The checklist may be useful for readers interested in understanding and tracking the high-level steps of the process, as the remainder of this report provides detailed guidance for implementing those steps. Since the checklist maps to the phases of the CMTA process and, in turn, the chapters and sections of this report, the reader can easily refer back to sections of this document as more detail is needed.

2. Phase One: Establishing CMTA Roles and Analysis Inputs

Before the CMTA can be planned or executed, the roles and responsibilities of the involved organizations and personnel should be established and the scope of the CMTA effort should be defined, taking into consideration the resources and time available. These roles include the executing organization, analyst team members, and internal and external SMEs. In addition to having responsibilities to carry out the CMTA process, the analyst team and SMEs provide information as inputs to the analysis. That is, to build the mission thread and rank the criticality of systems to the mission, specific information is needed. This information may originate from many sources including relevant mission and system reference documents (e.g., operational architectures) and SMEs internal and external to the executing organization, as well as the analyst team members themselves. Each analysis input (i.e., documentation, SMEs, and analyst team) should be carefully selected such that a comprehensive picture of the operational mission and systems can be constructed. Duplication of informational areas among analysis inputs may sometimes be necessary (e.g., operators should validate whether architectures are current and correct). However, the number of members on the analyst team and SMEs should be selected with a desire to optimize the efficiency of the process and minimize the collective resources and level of effort needed.

In this chapter, we discuss how to establish the roles and responsibilities of the CMTA stakeholders and gather and review relevant reference documents to ensure that the proper analysis inputs are available. The initial assumption for this first phase of the CMTA process is that the mission and the concepts of operations for analysis have been identified and scoped, as described in Snyder et al. (2022), and thus the relevant operational concepts and systems are at least identifiable, if not well understood yet. An additional assumption is that a CMTA process owner has been chosen by U.S. Air Force leadership to manage the overall process for all missions and has resources to support CMTA exercises. In this role, the CMTA process owner orchestrates the overall timing of CMTA exercises and gathers lessons learned from each to institutionalize them for future exercises. The CMTA process owner also plays a key role in securing the availability of SMEs from organizations outside its chain of command and SME buy-in for the process, as discussed in Chapter 3. Finally, the CMTA process owner should explain the objectives of CMTA to organizations that execute the process. This effort could include an explanation of the CMTA deliverables and a description of the expected format and level of detail of the final mission thread and system ranking.[1]

---

[1] One effective way to communicate the level of detail and indenture needed to successfully complete the CMTA is for the CMTA process owner to provide an example mission thread. This could either be a completed, high-quality mission thread or a simple exemplar mission thread—one that is small in scope and generic enough that no expertise is necessary.

The timeline for completing tasks described in this chapter is uncertain and depends on a number of situational factors, such as the availability of SMEs, existing relationships between the CMTA process owner and the executing and external SME organizations, how long it takes the executing organization to build a team, and whether analyst team members are available to start work right away. Therefore, we estimate that this phase could take anywhere from one week to one month to complete. In Chapter 5 we discuss efficiencies that may be adopted to reduce the timeline of this phase.

Selecting an Executing Organization

While the CMTA process owner manages the overall process for all missions, a single organization should manage each CMTA at the mission level. This executing organization should, in general, be distinct from, but selected by, the CMTA process owner. The executing organization is in charge of assembling and overseeing the analyst team. Therefore, it should have expertise in the specific U.S. Air Force mission and systems under consideration. If selecting the analyst team from within its organization, it also needs to have the resources available to begin work in the time frame and at the level of effort necessary and the personnel to fill the various roles needed on the analyst team, as described in the next section.

U.S. Air Force operational organizations could be considered for the role of executing organization. They have strong in-house understanding of the mission and the operational roles and workarounds, but they may be burdened with potential biases and possible shortcomings in understanding the systems at a technical level.[2] They are also unlikely to have much experience with the more specialized aspects, such as process mapping, which may be more familiar to systems engineers. Additionally, the demands of operational obligations might limit the resources operational commands can devote to such an effort. In those cases where the operational command has shortfalls in expertise or availability, the analyst team roles can be filled with personnel cross-assigned from other government organizations, federally funded research and development centers, or support contractors, while remaining under the direction of the operational command.

Assembling the Analyst Team

The analyst team is selected by the executing organization. This team performs the majority of the work, planning and performing the CMTA. Collectively, the team requires knowledge of

- the operational mission and ideally engineering details of systems
- the CMTA process
- interviewing and/or group facilitation methods

---

[2] Program office personnel typically have this necessary technical expertise, but a number of missions will likely require systems expertise that spans across multiple programs.

- process mapping (i.e., ability to build the flow diagram of the mission thread in appropriate software such as Vizio or Sparx Enterprise Architecture)
- the system ranking technique and required tool(s).

While each team member may have more than one of these areas of expertise, we suggest that specific individuals be assigned the following roles:

- *Team leader.* This individual has a good understanding of the CMTA process and its objectives, familiarity with the pertinent mission and systems, and good management and sound communication skills.
- *Facilitator/interviewer.* The person in this role also has a good understanding of the CMTA process and its objectives and, importantly, is well versed or trainable in interview and group facilitation methods to keep discussions focused and on track without introducing bias or errors. While the facilitator/interviewer does not require the same level of knowledge about the mission area and systems as the other team members, this person should have enough competency to effectively and credibly interact with the SMEs, as well as to understand enough to keep discussions focused on relevant information.
- *Process mapper.* This role requires someone who is trained or trainable to develop the functional flow block diagram that will represent the mission thread using process mapping software, as exemplified in Snyder et al. (2022).[3]
- *SME engagement note-taker.* This individual should have sufficient subject-matter expertise to capture all relevant information.

As the roles of the team leader and facilitator/interviewer are so crucial to the success of the CMTA, they may best be assigned to two separate team members for which that is their sole role.[4]

Each team member may have multiple responsibilities. The team leader's responsibility encompasses overseeing the CMTA process and the analyst team, as well as interfacing with the leadership of the executing organization and the CMTA process owner. The team leader makes the final decision on the end product of the CMTA and as such should be involved in decisionmaking at each phase of the process. This team leader may also be the lead on all analyses conducted by the analyst team. For example, once SME inputs have been collected to inform mission thread development, we envision the team leader running a working meeting among the analyst team to determine how to use those inputs and build the initial mission thread.

While the team leader manages the analyst team, the facilitator/interviewer manages all interactions with the external SMEs. In this way, external SMEs have only one point of contact—the person who recruits them is also the one who facilitates meetings they attend and

---

[3] More detailed information on process mapping, specifically functional analysis can be found in Viola et al. (2012) and in chapter 5 of Leonard (2001).

[4] This is also suggested by the Air Force Materiel Command Office of Aerospace Studies (2014) when assembling the high-performance teams to conduct an analysis of alternatives (AoA).

sends the emails with questionnaires for them to fill out. Such a role improves trust and rapport between the SMEs and facilitator.

The other team members may analyze the available documentation and determine what information needs to be elicited from the internal and external SMEs to generate and refine the mission thread and produce a system ranking; observe and document the information gathered during the SME engagements; and construct the mission thread and undertake the system ranking and triage assessment. Finally, given the anticipated pace of the analysis and engagements with SMEs, it is useful if one team member familiar with the analysis serves as an official note-taker during interactions with the SMEs, augmented by the analyst team members in attendance also taking notes during SME engagements.

While there is no set size for the analyst team, the composition of the team would benefit from covering all of the required responsibilities while not being so large that scheduling working meetings with the entire analyst team becomes challenging.[5]

Gathering and Reviewing Relevant Documents

With an analyst team assembled, the team can begin to initiate the major tasks in the CMTA process. Appendix B is a checklist for the analyst team to follow that mirrors the narrative in the remainder of this report and provides administrative details for the team to consider.

The analyst team's first task as part of the CMTA process is to gather and review relevant mission and systems documentation. As the team collects this information, it should keep in mind the level of detail needed to complete CMTA—that is, documents only need to have detail to build a mission thread good enough to rank system criticality. Documents (and the resulting mission thread) do not need to provide information to produce an exhaustive flow diagram of the mission.

Documents collected may include Department of Defense Architecture Framework (DoDAF) artifacts, including the operations view (i.e., OV-1 and OV-6) and systems view (i.e., SV-1 and SV-6).[6] Given that these are common across all programs, if they are up to date, these artifacts provide a consistent view of operational and system architectures. Dated architectures should be consulted with caution and augmented by SME input. Fortunately, additional documents may help the analyst team gain an understanding of the mission and systems, such as systems engineering artifacts. A list of all the documents to consider is included in the checklist in Appendix B.

While the team can later use the mission and systems documents to build the initial mission thread, at this stage their main purpose is to help the team decide what areas of expertise need to

---

[5] In an initial CMTA exercise carried out by RAND for the flight line maintenance support of aircraft sortie generation, a team of only four individuals sufficed to successfully carry out the effort (Lynch, 2017).

[6] For guidance on these and other DoDAF viewpoints, see DoD CIO (2017).

be covered by SMEs. Therefore, the first review of these documents could produce a list of mission areas and systems for which quality, detailed information does not exist. The team can use this list, along with other inputs as described in the following section, to determine the areas of expertise for which SMEs are needed.

Identifying and Recruiting SMEs

Mission and system SMEs are the final set of CMTA stakeholders that need to be assembled, and their selection is a task charged to the analyst team. To do this, the analyst team can first identify gaps in expertise and knowledge that will guide SME selection. The team can then determine the organizations that may house this expertise and knowledge and reach out to those organizations to secure their buy-in, and then identify and recruit specific individuals who can act as CMTA SMEs. Each step of this process is discussed in detail below.

Determining Gaps in Expertise

As discussed at the beginning of this chapter, information from SMEs makes up one of the important analysis inputs, with the other two being the expertise of the analyst team and relevant documentation. To determine the SMEs that are needed for a CMTA, the analyst team can conduct an inventory of the current expertise and knowledge available (e.g., maintenance, situational awareness, sortie generation). This inventory might be compared against the expertise needed to properly conduct the CMTA to determine gaps that need to be filled by SMEs. When developing this inventory, the analyst team members should consider how confident they are that the information source is accurate, current, and complete. If they lack full confidence in an information source, they might conservatively denote this as a gap in expertise.

To develop a list of expertise needed to properly conduct the analysis, the analyst team should consider two main categories: system-independent activities that take place during the operation of the mission, and technical and engineering knowledge of all the systems used during mission operations.[7] Mission-level knowledge includes high-level support functions and detailed operational processes. Additional knowledge of available operational workarounds, as well as their impact on mission effectiveness, is also necessary. System-level knowledge includes both depth, for a good understanding of the technical details of the subsystems, and breadth, for the integrative perspective. Additional knowledge about current and potential future system vulnerabilities is beneficial.

Before reaching out to external SMEs, the analyst team should consider what expertise is available in-house, within the executing organization. These "internal SMEs" should be vetted as to whether their knowledge is current. If so, this could reduce the number of external SMEs that

---

[7] If the mission scope includes command, control, and communications functions, the analyst team may additionally consider SMEs with expertise in network administration and/or operation.

the analyst team needs to recruit. However, when choosing the balance of internal and external SMEs, the analyst team may choose to conservatively include enough external SMEs so that the SME critical review activities still provide a source of independent feedback.

Identifying Relevant SME Organizations

Once the gaps in areas of expertise have been identified, the next proposed step for the analyst team is to identify the SME organizations that can speak to those areas. We expect SMEs to come from two primary communities: the operational community to inform the operational and sustainment activities and identification of systems used to perform these activities, and the engineering and systems community to inform the analysis of systems supporting the mission. Individuals in the operational community can typically be found in the operational wings of the U.S. Air Force major command mission-owners. Depending on the mission, representation from maintenance, support, or medical groups may be needed. Individuals in the engineering and systems community will typically reside within the associated program offices and their contractors, with lead subsystems engineers ideally situated to provide depth and systems engineers ideally situated to provide breadth. Knowledge about system vulnerabilities typically resides with the lead subsystems and systems engineers or with the system-security engineers within the program offices, if such a role exists. Because numerous systems combine to perform any given mission, SMEs from multiple program offices may in general need to participate.

When developing a list of SME organizations to contact, the analyst team should consider the benefits of obtaining diverse experts to ensure the analysis is thoroughly considered from many viewpoints.[8] Diversity follows from reaching out to many different communities (e.g., multiple wings, multiple contractors), as well as by including various experience levels, specifically up to instructor-level individuals if available. That said, the SMEs need not be equally drawn from the operational and engineering communities: In a pilot CMTA experience, the analyst team favored reaching out to external operational SMEs since much of the relevant systems engineering expertise was available in-house (MITRE, 2017).

Securing SME Organization Buy-In and Recruiting Individuals

To recruit individual SMEs, the leadership at their respective organizations will likely first need to be engaged. Without leadership buy-in from the organizations supplying the SMEs, there is a risk that SMEs might not be fully committed to the process. One way this buy-in can be obtained is by having the CMTA process owner or someone with comparable rank first contact the commanding officer (CO) or leadership of the SME organization.

When introducing the CMTA process and working with the CO/leadership to select SMEs, a few strategies may be helpful. First, while the mission thread analysis is cyber-focused, the

---

[8] For example, individuals in active duty, the reserves, and the National Guard may bring different perspectives on how to carry out mission tasks.

recruitment of SMEs could deemphasize the cyber aspect. Indeed, explicit knowledge about cyber is not required of the SMEs for success of the analysis, whereas knowledge of the mission, as well as the processes and systems enabling it, are essential. In other studies, we have found that the mention of cyber during the recruitment of relevant SMEs tends to result in taskings to network-related professionals instead of mission and system SMEs, even if mission- and system-level expertise is emphasized. Second, the CMTA process owner could stress the need for SMEs to be empowered to represent the organization. SMEs with in-depth and broad operational experience are needed. These personnel tend to be busy, so the analyst team should be wary of the SME organization volunteering personnel with better availability but with less expertise. To avoid this situation, the CMTA process owner might emphasize to the CO/leadership that the SME views will be understood to represent that of the SME organization, such that the organization will elect someone with the appropriate experience.

Once SMEs have been tasked by their CO/leadership, the facilitator/interviewer can contact them to better understand their specific expertise, any constraints they may have, such as conflicts of interest or biases, as well as their time availability. While we suggest that the same set of SMEs be used throughout the entire CMTA process, SME availability may change or new questions may arise that require different expertise. Therefore, some subset of the total SME pool may ultimately be chosen at the beginning of the process. Other SMEs may be advised that their expertise may be needed on an ad hoc basis. Since we propose that SMEs come together in a focus group, the number of SMEs may be best kept to no more than 12 participants to manage group discussions.[9] However, at least one to two SMEs from each area of expertise (e.g., maintenance, situational awareness, sortie generation) should be represented in the SME pool. For very complex missions, additional SMEs may be necessary.

Initial experience with executing a CMTA exercise indicated that the most significant driver of the duration of the exercise is the time needed to schedule and carry out SME engagements; these engagements typically took four to eight weeks from initial contact to when the engagements were carried out (MITRE, 2017). Therefore, initiating outreach to SMEs as soon as possible and conducting the outreach across SMEs in parallel rather than sequentially is critical to completing the CMTA exercise within the desired time frame.

---

[9] The ideal number of focus group participants is discussed further in Chapter 3.

3. Phase Two: Planning the Analysis Process

As depicted in Figure 1.1, the analysis process consists of four subphases: building the initial mission thread, critical review of that thread, ranking the systems, and critical review of the system ranking (and mission thread, as necessary). Included in these phases are tasks for the analyst team, internal and external SMEs, and leadership from the CMTA process owner and executing organization. Given the number of personnel involved and the desire for a streamlined process, it would be wise for the analyst team to create an analysis plan (and plan logistics accordingly) that outlines how and when the following activities take place: internal and external SME engagements, analyst team working meetings, and CMTA process owner and executing organization leadership feedback. The analyst team leader is well positioned to oversee this task, with SME engagement planning being the primary responsibility of the facilitator/interviewer. In this chapter, we provide background and suggestions for the development of such an analysis plan. Chapter 4 describes a proposed analysis plan to execute phase three of the CMTA process.

As with the first phase of the CMTA process, the timeline for completing tasks described in this chapter is uncertain and depends on a number of situational factors, such as the analyst team's prior experience with building an analysis plan and the ability of the team to reuse the analysis plan and SME engagement materials developed for CMTAs of previous missions. Therefore, we estimate that this phase could take anywhere from one week to one month to complete. One additional consideration for the planning phase is whether the analyst team has access to, and is trained in, the necessary tools for CMTA, such as process mapping software. Obtaining and training on appropriate tools could further increase the timeline for the planning phase. In Chapter 5 we discuss efficiencies that could be adopted to reduce the timeline of this phase.

Developing the Analysis Plan

The analysis plan, developed by the analyst team, will ultimately determine the schedule of the activities to take place as part of the CMTA. When developing this plan, the analyst team may benefit from considering a number of situational factors that may be difficult to change, including the following:

- *Internal knowledge of the mission and associated systems.* The extent of knowledge of the analyst team and relevant documentation will affect the completeness of the analyst team's initial understanding of mission thread map and system ranking. The greater the knowledge of the mission and systems, the less information the analyst team needs to elicit from SMEs. This consideration should include the quality of the relevant documentation (e.g., how current, accurate, and complete).
- *Number and availability of internal and external SMEs.* The analyst team should also consider the number and background of SMEs from which information will need to be

elicited. This information will be important when choosing the type of elicitation (e.g., interviews, focus groups, surveys), the mode of elicitation (e.g., in person, by phone, or online/email), and the number of elicitation engagements. Focus groups, for example, work best when the number of participants is limited to about a dozen; larger SME pools might be best handled with multiple focus groups (Dalal et al., 2011). The availability and location of external SMEs will also affect how information is elicited from them. Given that external SMEs will have limited time for the CMTA, it is likely impracticable for them to participate in and travel to more than one in-person focus group, in which case interviews by phone or at the SME job location may be needed.

- *Mission complexity.* The complexity of the mission will affect the facilitator/interviewer and analyst team's knowledge of the mission and the number of SMEs needed, as addressed previously. A complex mission, such as one where there are variations in how it might be executed (e.g., according to theater), could be a consideration in how SMEs are engaged.

- *Desired timeline.* The type of SME elicitation and mode of communication may differ depending on the CMTA process owner's timeline requirements. If SME numbers are large, questionnaires and focus groups, for instance, may require less time than one-on-one interviews. Additionally, an extended timeline may be needed to find a date in which all SMEs can attend a common focus group. Instead, multiple focus subgroups may allow for speedier scheduling.

By this phase in the CMTA process, most of the constraints in the list above are at least partially known. As discussed, each consideration has implications for the type and mode of SME engagements. Therefore, when building the analysis plan, the analyst team can begin by choosing the type and mode of SME engagement for each of the four subphases in the analysis. In the next two sections, we provide additional considerations for making this choice. This is followed by a brief discussion of the mode of other analyst team activities, including internal meetings, as well as interactions with internal SMEs within the executing organization.

Choosing the Type of SME Engagements

While a large number of methods exist to elicit information from SMEs, in this section we highlight those most likely to be used in the CMTA setting. In this setting, SMEs are primarily consulted to explore a topic (e.g., maintenance operations) or to confirm and correct information the analyst team presents (e.g., a completed mission thread). The information being elicited is qualitative in nature and requires that SMEs be uninhibited in the format of their responses. For this type of exploratory research, the most appropriate form of SME elicitation includes exploratory interviewing and focus groups (Babbie, 2007). As we later discuss, these types of SME engagements require phone calls, video teleconferencing, or in-person meetings. To provide the analyst team with more flexibility in the mode of communication, we also describe open-ended questionnaires, which can be completed through email correspondence but still provide a less inhibited form for SME responses. Table 3.1 summarizes the advantages and limitations of the three SME engagement types discussed in this section.

Table 3.1. Advantages and Limitations of the SME Engagement Types

	Exploratory Interviews	Focus Groups	Open-Ended Questionnaires
Time/resource commitments	Analyst team time and resource commitments increase proportional to the number of respondents	More efficient use of analyst team time and resources, but may require increased SME time commitments	Least time- and resource-intensive for both SMEs and the analyst team
Group interaction	No issues with group dynamics	Susceptible to group process losses, but group interactions may lead to consensus or easier identification of disagreements	No issues with group dynamics
Follow-up questioning	Allows for follow-up questions	Allows for follow-up questions	Does not easily allow for follow-up questions
Documentation	Note-taker required; possibility for concepts being lost in translation	Note-taker required; possibility for concepts being lost in translation	No note-taker required; documentation is provided in the SME's own words, reducing possibility of concepts being lost in translation
Mode of communication	Phone interviewing is usually sufficient and does not require travel	In-person focus groups may be most effective, but require travel by the analyst team and/or SMEs; using videoconferencing would preclude travel but may lead to group dynamic issues	May be sent via email or conducted online, requiring no travel
Coordination	Moderate logistical planning required, but multiple interviews must be planned	Only one meeting may be needed if SME numbers are small, but significant logistical planning is required	Little logistical planning required
Flexibility for SME availability	Moderately flexible to accommodate availability of SMEs	Once focus group date is set, no flexibility for SMEs	Most flexible for SMEs' availability

SOURCES: Babbie, 2007; Lazar, Feng, and Hochheiser, 2010; Robson, 2002; Harrell and Bradley, 2009; Morgan and Henrion, 1990; Fowler, 1995; Straus, Parker, and Bruce, 2011.

Exploratory Interviewing

An exploratory interview is an interaction between an interviewer and one or more respondents in which the plan of inquiry and topics to be covered are determined ahead of time but the interviewer's questions are only loosely prepared (Babbie, 2007). Two forms of exploratory interviews may be needed in the CMTA process: semi-structured and open-ended. While semi-structured interviews follow a script, the interviewer may ask follow-up and clarifying questions (Lazar, Feng, and Hochheiser, 2010). Open-ended interviews are more exploratory in nature and generally guided by only discussion points, with suggested formulations for questioning (Robson, 2002). Open-ended interviews are usually conducted when it is important not to prime the respondent with information, which can bias their responses (Morgan et al., 2002). As we discuss in detail in Appendix A, open-ended interview protocols can be useful when the analyst team has minimal knowledge about (portions of) the mission thread and wants to elicit a step-by-step process of mission operations from SMEs without biasing them as to what that process may look like. Semi-structured interviews, on the other hand, can be useful when probing on a specific branch of the mission thread for which the analyst team only needs clarifying information. Suggested wording for questions an interviewer may use are also provided in Appendix A.

Exploratory interviewing is an effective means to eliciting the type of information from SMEs needed for the CMTA context. When interviewing a single respondent, there is an opportunity to discuss information one-on-one with the SME, which prevents a number of group dynamics issues that can arise in focus groups, such as overlooking minority viewpoints.[1] Unlike questionnaires, interviewing additionally allows an interviewer to ask follow-up and clarifying questions that would ensure the analyst team has a complete understanding of the SME's perspective. However, one-on-one exploratory interviews can be time- and resource-intensive: In addition to the time required of the interviewer to conduct the interview, a separate note-taker should be present, and the notes must be cleaned and analyzed after the interview takes place. If the number of SMEs is large, one-hour interviews with each can easily become multiple person-days of effort (Lazar, Feng, and Hochheiser, 2010; Robson, 2002).

Focus Groups

A focus group is a dynamic group discussion led by a facilitator and characterized by interactions among participants (Morgan, 1997). Focus groups tend to be somewhere between semi-structured and unstructured in nature, allowing enough freedom for participants to comment on each other's responses but structured enough to ensure that the group remains in scope and covers the pertinent discussion topics. The group interaction provides a means for participants to gain feedback on their responses, which may lead them to negotiate toward consensus or identify areas in which conflicting opinions or uncertainty exists (Harrell and Bradley, 2009; Morgan and Henrion, 1990). In this way, focus groups may be helpful during critical review of the initial mission thread, providing an effective means for the analyst team to clarify areas of divergence found during the first SME elicitation (e.g., are conflicting SME responses two ways of saying the same thing or are they indicative of two different workarounds in a mission thread branch?). Suggestions for a focus group schedule and questions in the CMTA context are provided in Appendix A.

As with all SME elicitation methods, focus groups have their advantages and limitations. First, depending on the number of SMEs, a group setting may be a more efficient use of the analyst team's time. The analyst team only needs to plan one meeting and all SME inputs are collected during it. Focus groups, however, necessitate careful planning and design. From a logistics perspective, scheduling a time (likely to be at least a day or more in the CMTA context) and place (if holding in-person focus groups) for all necessary SMEs to meet may be difficult and may even delay the CMTA schedule. From a procedural point of view, a well-trained

---

[1] These and other group process losses are discussed further in Appendix A.

facilitator is required for keeping the conversation on track, promoting balanced respondent participation, and eliminating bias, as discussed further in Appendix A (Harrell and Bradley, 2009). Additionally, more than one focus group or breakout sessions within a larger focus group may be necessary if the number of SMEs is large. Some researchers recommend that the optimal focus group size is eight to 12 participants (Robson, 2002) while others recommend smaller groups of five to seven participants (Krueger and Casey, 2014). A focus group on the larger end of this range will result in each SME having less time to speak and more opportunity for the facilitator to lose control of the conversation and the issues that may arise because of group dynamics, as discussed further in Appendix A (Straus, Parker, and Bruce, 2011). The group dynamic can be as much a negative as a positive in some circumstances. Focus groups that are monopolized by individuals or encounter power struggles and conflict may reduce the reliability of the insights gleaned (Lazar, Feng, and Hochheiser, 2010). The facilitator should be aware of such dynamics and adjust the group toward fair participation.

Open-Ended Questionnaires

As an alternative to interviews and focus groups, which must be done in person, over the phone, or via videoconference, open-ended questionnaires are surveys that can be distributed and collected by email[2] and allow respondents to provide their answers in narrative format (Fowler, 1995). This type of SME engagement provides the analyst team with the most flexibility—the analyst team emails the questionnaire to the SMEs, designates a deadline for responses, and compiles results once all questionnaires have been received. It is also the least resource-intensive of the three SME engagement types we discuss. One additional benefit of open-ended questionnaires is that SME responses are recorded (and can be referred back to) in their own words, resulting in fewer ideas getting lost or misconstrued in translation by a note-taker.

In our opinion, these benefits do not outweigh the limitations of using open-ended questionnaires for the purposes of CMTA. No matter how well crafted the questions are, the analyst team's inability to ask clarifying questions or probe for additional insights that could be discovered along the way (Babbie, 2007) make this type of SME engagement the least desirable. Additionally, busy SMEs may overlook emailed questionnaires or not respond in a timely manner. For this reason, their use may be best only during the final stage of critical review, once the analyst team is relatively confident it has an accurate mission thread and system ranking. In Appendix A, we provide guidance on relevant questions. An open-ended questionnaire at this stage would allow SMEs to review the CMTA results, confirm that nothing is missing or inaccurate, and provide specific feedback (e.g., to portions of the mission thread or a certain system's ranking) that the analyst team can use either to tweak results or to document areas of uncertainty. If open-ended questionnaires must be used to inform the initial mission thread, we

---

[2] As an alternative to emailing a questionnaire, the analyst team can develop an online survey and send SMEs a link.

suggest that the analyst team hold informal follow-up phone calls or email exchanges with select SMEs in order to have an opportunity to clarify issues and probe deeper into topics.

Choosing the Mode of SME Engagements

When developing the analysis plan, the analyst team should consider the benefits and challenges of the different modes of SME engagement. A questionnaire could most likely be administered by email, but exploratory interviews and focus groups could each take place on the phone, via videoconference, or in person. The primary benefit of using email for SME engagement is that respondents can provide answers at the time of their choosing, but busy engineers or operators may also overlook or incompletely answer the email, as they find discussing a topic easier than writing about it, thereby presenting a challenge to meeting the CMTA timelines. Scheduling SME engagements (i.e., interviews or focus groups) by phone, videoconference, or in person, however, is more likely to convey the importance of the engagement and improve response rates and timelines.

In our experience, engaging SMEs in person is the best way to gain their trust, ensure their commitment, and receive their buy-in of the results. Of course, in-person meetings may require travel by SMEs and/or the analyst team, and coordination of schedules may delay CMTA timelines. This trade-off requires the analyst team to consider the relative benefit of conducting interviews or focus groups in person versus by videoconference or telephone. In the case of focus groups, the relative benefit to the group interaction appears to be large. Nonverbal communication between focus group members is almost as important as verbal communication (Harrell and Bradley, 2009). Group interactions also tend to change in videoconference and audioconference settings—participants tend to form local coalitions with those in the same room, disagreeing more with those on the other end of the connection (Wainfan and Davis, 2004). For these reasons, conducting focus groups in person may produce the best results.

In the case of exploratory interviewing, in-person meetings are still ideal because they allow the interviewer to go beyond verbal language and to observe nonverbal cues and body language (Lazar, Feng, and Hochheiser, 2010). Such interactions may be possible if the interview takes place as a videoconference, but this mode of engagement requires the technology be available and compatible for both the analyst team and SME. An additional benefit of in-person interviews over videoconferencing is that SMEs can print out relevant documentation, place it on a table in front of them, and walk through it with the analyst team. While these advantages to in-person interviewing have significance, the purpose of the SME engagements for CMTA is informational, so nonverbal cues may be less important than in instances where interviews cover sensitive topics. Furthermore, relevant documentation can always be emailed to analyst team members before the interview. The primary argument for in-person interviewing, then, is to gain the trust and buy-in of SMEs. Therefore, if the analyst team plans to conduct in-person focus groups at other times during the CMTA process, exploratory interviews may be conducted over the phone or via videoconference to increase the efficiency of the process.

Determining Other Analyst Team Activities

Once the type and mode of SME engagements have been chosen, the analyst team should also determine the activities that take place internally at the executing organization. These include analyst team activities to (1) develop the analysis plan and plan logistics, (2) build the mission thread and identify relevant systems for ranking, (3) refine the mission thread and systems after critical review, (4) conduct the system rankings, (5) refine the system rankings after critical review, (6) finalize CMTA results, and (7) document lessons learned. These analyst team activities may be formal or informal—that is, a working meeting can be planned with a set agenda or one analyst team member can take the lead on an activity and hold impromptu meetings with other team members. Many of these activities could likely benefit from a more structured meeting setting in which the team members with various areas of expertise are all represented, a member is assigned to take notes (allowing for ease of future documentation), and a clear objective for the meeting is communicated. While holding structured working meetings for each activity may be effective, it is probably not efficient. Finding a time when (a subset of) the entire team can attend a meeting for the better part of the day may be difficult if team members have other responsibilities. Therefore, as with the SME engagements, the analyst team must consider the trade-offs when planning internal analyst team activities.

Another analyst team activity that takes place internally at the executing organization is interaction with internal SMEs. These interactions can be undertaken with exploratory interviews or open-ended questionnaires, similar to external SME engagements. Interviews may occur in person or by videoconference if these colleagues work in different locations. The use of focus groups is less likely to be necessary as the number of internal SMEs and the diversity of their viewpoints will likely be fewer. The same advantages and limitations discussed for the type and mode of SME engagements apply to these internal SME activities. However, engagements with colleagues may be less formal than those with external SMEs, as internal SMEs may already be acquainted with members of the analyst team and may be more accessible for asking follow-up questions—for example, through unscheduled visits to their office. For these reasons, in-person or phone interviews with internal SMEs can be used to inform the mission thread. The interview protocol developed for external SMEs may be reused with internal SMEs. Critical review activities with internal SMEs may be performed most efficiently as emailed questionnaires that resemble those that will be used with external SMEs.

Additional analyst team activities worth noting are interactions with the CMTA process owner and executing organization leadership. The analyst team could perform a critical review of the mission thread and system ranking with these two CMTA stakeholders. This critical review ensures that the analyst's execution of the analysis is credible from the senior leadership's perspective, that CMTA results remain in scope of the mission (and concepts of operations) and produce the correct level of detail (e.g., the mission thread should produce a list of relevant

21

systems, though levels of indenture below this may be unnecessary), and that the analyst team is correctly applying lessons learned from past CMTAs.

One final set of analyst activities, which will be discussed in detail in Chapter 5, is the documentation of lessons learned. The learning curve can be accelerated if the analyst team formally documents lessons learned. This product could be a required deliverable when an executing organization submits CMTA results, especially for the first tranche of missions assessed. These lessons learned could include those related to the preparation or the implementation of the analysis, as well as submissions of SME engagement materials developed and used.

Planning Logistics and Preparing Materials

The proposed analysis plan moves at a swift pace. Every detail should be planned in advance—from the development of questionnaires and SME handouts to the reservation of meeting rooms or conference lines for SME engagements. This logistical planning should occur before the analysis begins. In this section, we detail the most important aspects of logistical planning.

As further detailed in the checklist in Appendix B, the facilitator/interviewer can begin by scheduling the SME engagements. Complementary to this action, a member of the analyst team can then schedule the analyst team working meetings. Furthermore, briefings of interim CMTA results to the CMTA process owner and executing organization leadership can also be scheduled in advance. Finally, the facilitator/interviewer should be responsible for overseeing the activities and finalizing the interview and focus group protocols and questionnaire and SME handout development. This may take some time the first time these materials are developed, but future analyses may then use the originals as a template. The initial development of protocols and questionnaires could be pilot-tested ahead of time with a small number SMEs. This is discussed further in Appendix A.

4. Phase Three: Conducting the Analysis

With all CMTA stakeholders in place and preparations made, the analyst team can finally perform the analysis. The analysis phase includes four subphases: Build the initial mission thread, review the thread, rank and triage systems, and review and finalize the CMTA results. In this chapter, we describe each subphase and offer generalized suggestions on how to conduct the activities that take place during each, as depicted in the proposed analysis plan shown in Figure 4.1. The figure provides one way of implementing phase three functions of the CMTA process. All four subphases are represented in the analysis plan, as shown on the left-hand side of the figure. The analysis plan is envisioned as a six-week process if all activities stay on schedule. If the schedule slips, some time may be recuperated by adjusting the methods using one of the time-saving strategies discussed later in this chapter.

Figure 4.1. A Proposed Analysis Plan and Timeline for Phase Three (Conducting the Analysis)

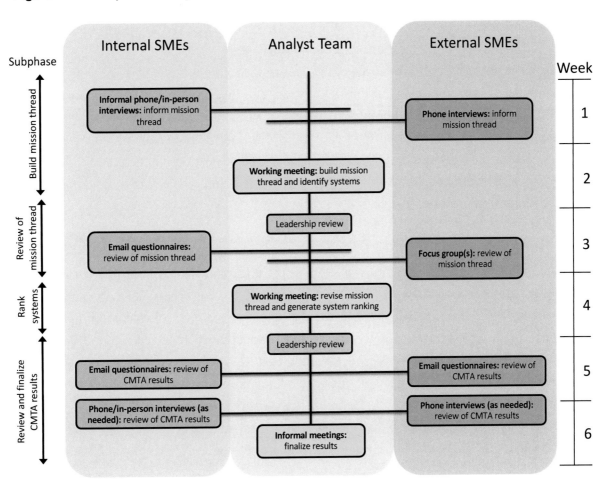

The proposed analysis plan uses multiple SME elicitation methods in a specific sequence (interviews followed by focus groups, then finally questionnaires). The use of multiple methods, in the sequence shown, is deliberate and each week's activities are dependent on those in the previous week (see Figure 1.1 for a full mapping of dependencies). Interviews act as an exploratory tool for eliciting the mission thread in depth. Focus groups then allow for iterative refinement of the thread. Finally, questionnaires provide a means for SMEs to provide confirmatory comments, which can be used to gauge the prevalence of SMEs' approval. Engaging SMEs in a mixed-methods approach is a common approach for information elicitation (Harrell and Bradley, 2009; Morgan et al., 2002). When the analyst team develops its analysis plan, it may be worth considering a mixed-methods sequence accordingly.

Developing the Initial Mission Thread

The objective of this substage is to develop an initial mission thread map that graphically relates the overall mission, mission functions, and systems, as detailed further in Snyder et al. (2022). This ultimately produces a list of systems that will later be ranked according to a set of criticality criteria. An additional objective of this substage could be to draft a list of remaining questions about, and issues with, the mission thread. This could be used to inform future questions for SMEs during the next critical review substage.

To reach the objectives of this substage, the analyst team might begin by reviewing relevant documentation and drawing on any in-house knowledge of the mission area and supporting systems that the analyst team or internal SMEs possess. Next, the analyst team could elicit information about the mission thread from external SMEs as well. Subsequently, the team could collate and review all information it has on the mission and relevant systems (e.g., SME interview notes, relevant documentation). Finally, the team could convene to build the mission thread and identify outstanding issues.

Eliciting Information from SMEs

Depending on the quality, breadth, and depth of the information readily available to the analyst team members, they may benefit from eliciting information from SMEs about the mission thread. To do this, the analyst team could conduct phone interviews with both internal and external SMEs. The analyst team could target to conduct these interviews in one week unless the number of SMEs is large or there are scheduling issues.

We expect that these SME inputs will originate both from their past experience and knowledge as well as reference documents such as technical manuals to which only these SMEs may have access. The analyst team should encourage SMEs to rely on all sources when providing information about the mission and, if permitted, to share reference documents with the analyst team.

Before eliciting any information from SMEs, the facilitator could provide them (via email) with some introductory materials and direct the SMEs to review and bring along to the session any relevant documentation. If using interviews to engage both internal and external SMEs, the less formal discussions with internal SMEs can be conducted first. This provides the interviewer an opportunity to try out the interview protocol on a "friendly face" and to work out any issues in the questioning. If engagement is performed through questionnaires, both internal and external SMEs likely need to be queried concurrently to keep within the analysis plan's timeline. We provide further details of how to perform these interviews in Appendix A.

While the interviewer should facilitate the discussion, a note-taker knowledgeable about the mission area should be capturing the necessary substance of what the SME is stating. After all interviews are complete, the note-taker and interviewer can then take the time to briefly analyze the findings. This analysis can include a summary of the major themes found across SMEs,[1] any contradictory information or disagreements between SMEs, and any areas that need clarification or further questioning. This analysis serves two functions: It provides other analyst team members with a summary of the major findings of the interview, and it is a succinct means of documenting the interviews that can be easily reviewed at a later date. Further administrative suggestions for eliciting information from SMEs can be found in the checklist in Appendix B.

Sketching the Initial Mission Thread

At this juncture, the analyst team is ready to develop the initial mission thread. We propose that the team hold a working meeting that follows a set agenda and is led by the team leader. All members of the analyst team could be present and have reviewed interview notes and any relevant documentation. One team member at the meeting can develop a flow diagram using appropriate software, such as Vizio or Sparx Enterprise Architecture.[2] A generic format for a functional flow block diagram is shown in Figure 4.2. Thus, the mission thread can be built dynamically. The initial mission thread can be constructed over the course of a two-day working meeting. We estimate that preparations for the meeting (e.g., to collate and review notes and document results) could round out this activity to about a week.

The first objective of this meeting is to generate and agree on a breakdown of the mission into mission functions. The agenda for the remainder of the meeting may then be best organized by mission function. Discussions of each function may be allotted a specific amount of time. By the end of that time frame, the process mapper could have dynamically developed the mission thread branch for that function. Any areas of uncertainty, disagreements between team members, or points where clarification is needed could be documented. Ultimately, it is probably best that the team leader has the final decision in the development of the mission thread but that dissenting

---

[1] We direct readers interested in theme identification to Ryan and Bernard (2003).

[2] More detailed information on process mapping, specifically functional analysis, can be found in Viola et al. (2012) and in chapter 5 of Leonard (2001).

Figure 4.2. Generic Format of a Functional Flow Block Diagram

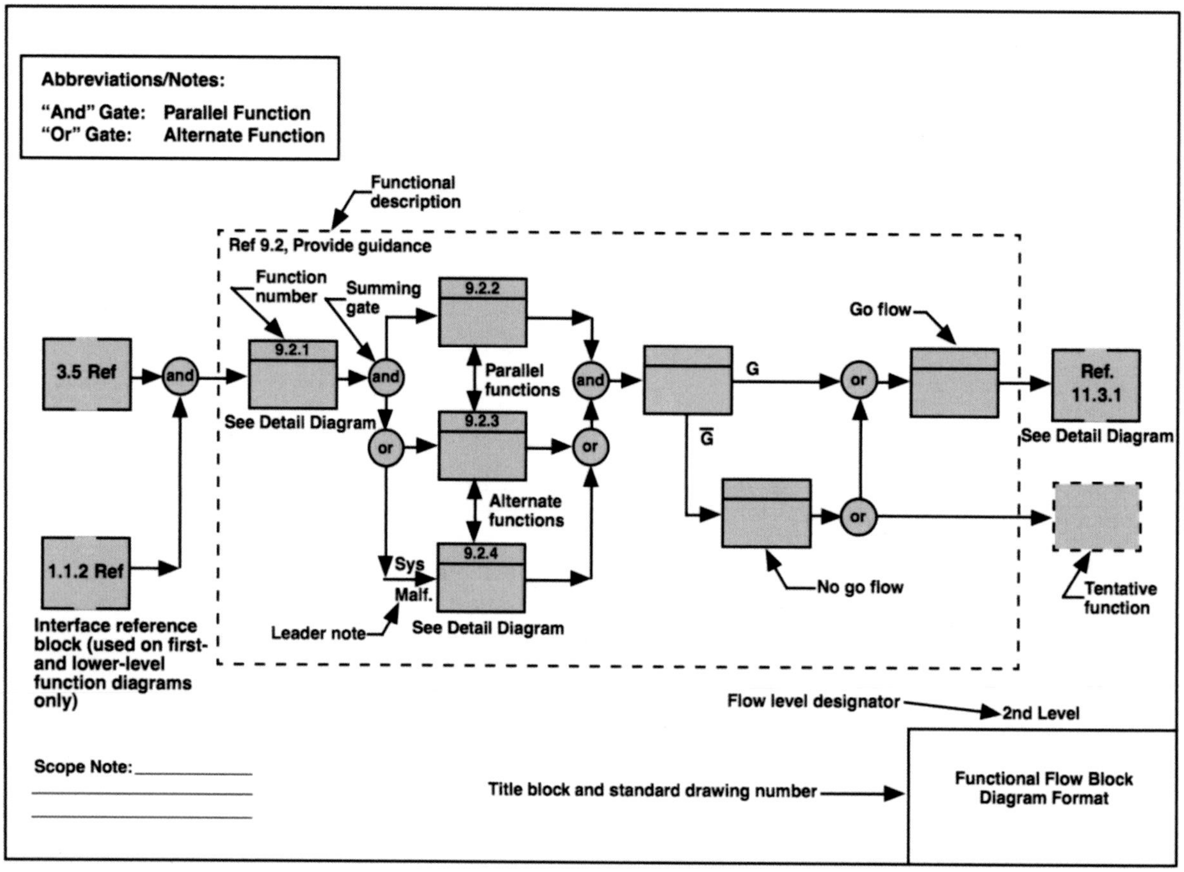

views or uncertainties be noted and addressed during the critical review subphase with SMEs and leadership. We stress the need to complete an initial mission thread within the meeting's time frame—even if incorrect in parts. The objective at this stage is not to have a perfect mission thread, but one for SMEs and leadership to review and provide feedback on and corrections during the critical review subphase.

Reviewing the Initial Mission Thread

The objectives of this substage are for (1) leadership of the executing organization and CMTA process owner to critically review and provide feedback on the scope and level of detail of the initial mission thread, (2) SMEs to critically review and provide feedback on the initial mission thread, and (3) the analyst team to revise the mission thread based on this feedback. We adopt the term "critical review" for the activities in this (and the final) substage to imply its purpose as objective and evaluative in nature. The analyst team should strive to make the CMTA products as accurate and useful as possible. CMTA stakeholder feedback can help with this goal. However, the critical review should not be implemented with the goal of receiving sign-off from all stakeholders. For example, coordination up the chain of command for this sign-off may be time-consuming and would also miss the point of this activity being one of evaluation.

To reach these objectives, the analyst team can conduct an in-person focus group with external SMEs and email questionnaires to internal SMEs, both focused on a critical review of the mission thread. Additionally, the analyst team can brief leadership from the CMTA process owner and the executing organization on the initial mission thread and elicit their feedback. Subsequently, the team might hold a second working meeting to revise the mission thread. In this section, we discuss the SME critical reviews and analyst team working meeting. The briefing to leadership should be implemented as deemed appropriate by the analyst team. However, we suggest the team elicit feedback on whether the mission thread remains in scope and provides the correct level of detail, as well as the credibility of the analysis plan—for example, by asking for feedback on the expertise of the SMEs included and the SME engagement activities chosen.

Conducting the SME Critical Reviews

External SME Focus Group

The primary activity in this substage is to hold a focus group with SMEs so that they can review and provide feedback on the initial mission thread. The focus group should be led by the facilitator/interviewer, ideally with most if not all analyst team members in attendance, including at least the note-taker and analyst team leader. While preferable to do so with everyone in one room, performing the SME engagement by videoconference or phone may be sufficient if the number of SMEs is small (e.g., four or fewer). We recommend, however, that the engagement take place in a manner that allows for interaction between SMEs (i.e., not through one-on-one interviews or questionnaires), as it is the best way for the analyst team to confirm consensus or discover any disagreements among SMEs. Assuming that SMEs receive and review the initial mission thread prior to the focus group, this critical review should be able to be completed within a day. If the number of SMEs is reasonably small (e.g., 12 or fewer), all SMEs can be gathered for one focus group. In this case, the focus group activity, including travel, could potentially be completed in one week. An additional focus group would likely add another week to this timeline.

Regardless of the mode of communication for the focus group, the facilitator may develop a protocol that ensures the group discusses the entire mission thread over the course of one to two (for very complex missions) days. This is no easy task, and therefore the facilitator should have a detailed plan before the group meeting date. If time permits, it would be beneficial to email the initial mission thread to the SMEs a few days before attending the focus group session.

During the focus group session, the facilitator can provide the SMEs with an agenda that allows time in the morning to review all of the emailed materials, including the initial mission thread. Next, the facilitator can engage SMEs in a discussion. The agenda could include a block of time to discuss each function in the mission (and the facilitator should hold to agenda times rather strictly) and finally a period of time at the end of the session for discussion of related but potentially overlooked topics.

Disagreements between SMEs identified during the focus group should be debated but not necessarily forced to consensus. The facilitator should make an effort to understand why these disagreements exist. For example, there are often variations in operational procedures carried out by active-duty personnel and the reserves versus the Air National Guard, or during war and peacetime. In these cases, the mission thread may need to be represented in a few different concepts of operations. In other cases, there may simply be two ways to do the same activity. Remember that the goal of CMTA is to identify and prioritize systems for further analysis, so both ways only need to be represented if new systems are identified or the mission thread might change enough to shift the criticality of existing systems. For further considerations and detailed recommendations on how to conduct the focus group, we direct the reader to Appendix A.

After the focus group has ended, the official note-taker captures relevant information in a similar manner to that completed in the previous subphase. Further administrative suggestions for conducting the external SME focus groups can be found in the checklist in Appendix B.

Internal SME Questionnaires

Depending on the extent and quality of internal SME inputs to the initial mission thread, the analyst team may also ask internal SMEs to provide a critical review at this juncture. A member of the analyst team could send an email to these SMEs that includes the initial mission thread followed by a set of open-ended questions. These questions can be structured in a format similar to that of the external SME focus group protocol—including a block of space devoted to each function of the mission. Internal SMEs can be queried about any activity or system that is missing, wrong, or confusing, and importantly, they can be asked how the mission thread could be revised to resolve the issue.

These questionnaires can be emailed to internal SMEs before the external SME focus group and their responses requested by the time the note-taker is summarizing focus group notes. In this way, internal SME inputs could be included in such summaries.

Revising the Initial Mission Thread

To revise the mission thread, the analyst team can hold another working meeting that follows a similar format to the meeting held to develop the initial mission thread, so the team can dynamically revise the thread in a systematic manner, function by function. Again, any areas of uncertainty, disagreements between team members, or points where clarification is needed should be documented. While the team leader should still be mindful of keeping to the meeting's time frame, unlike the initial mission thread development meeting, the objective of this meeting is to produce an accurate list of systems for prioritization even if the meeting time needs to be extended. We envision the working meeting lasting about two days. We estimate that preparations for the meeting (e.g., collating and reviewing questionnaires and notes, documenting results) could round out this activity to about a week.

Ranking Systems

The objective of this substage is to obtain a prioritized list of systems that are considered to be the most critical in terms of mission impact, as detailed in Snyder et al. (2022). The first step is to perform a cut set analysis, which should result in a first round of triage of the systems. This analysis can be determined for each system based solely on information included in the mission thread. Thus, the analyst team should be able to perform the analysis without inputs from SMEs or documentation, given the team has the proper tool and experience with or knowledge of how to use it. The tool needed to perform the cut set analysis, while outside the scope of this implementation guide,[3] could be as simple as a prepared Excel spreadsheet requiring analyst input or it can be a more complex tool that can analyze the actual flow diagram of the mission thread across a number of attributes, such as Sparx Enterprise Architecture.[4]

Next, if the prioritization needs to be refined further, the systems can be ranked in terms of a set of criticality criteria, such as the number of system dependencies or cyber separability. Snyder et al. (2022) suggests four such criticality criteria, but with experience these may be refined. Assigning criticality criteria values for each system mostly can be determined directly from the mission thread. For example, one scale proposed for cyber distance assigns values based on whether the system uses no computers, is a stand-alone machine, is an air-gapped machine, or is networked with a non-internet protocol. With criticality values assigned for each system, the analyst team can perform this ranking. To do so, the team should determine the relative importance of the criteria as well as a method for prioritizing systems against each criterion. For example, the analyst team may determine system dependencies and choose a cut-off value in which systems above a certain number of dependencies are then analyzed for the other criteria.

The analyst team may choose to conduct the criticality analysis during the working meeting for revising the mission thread. System rankings that result from the revised mission thread could be discussed. Surprising results could be mapped back to the mission thread and to the relative importance given to each criticality criteria as a means of understanding why certain systems may be ranked higher or lower than previously anticipated. Furthermore, if the criticality analysis can easily be updated, the analyst team may choose to analyze the sensitivity of results to remaining disagreements about the importance assigned to criteria or uncertainties within the mission thread. For example, if two SMEs disagree about the way a specific activity is represented

---

[3] As described in Chapter 1, the development of analytic tools for CMTA is a separate objective within LOA #1 and therefore is not included in this report.

[4] The timeline of the proposed analysis plan assumes such a tool already exists and the analyst team does not need to develop it.

in the mission thread or about the importance assigned to criteria, but both SMEs produce the same system ranking, the analyst team can confidently adopt one representation and merely document the other. Any disagreements between analyst team members might be settled by the team leader and can be noted in the final results.

Reviewing CMTA Results

The final subphase of the analysis involves the critical review of the system rankings and mission thread as necessary. As with the previous critical review, the analyst team should engage the SMEs to ensure that the results are consistent with their knowledge and experience and then brief the leadership of the CMTA process owner and executing organization to ensure the results are within scope and at the appropriate level of detail. Unlike the previous SME critical review, though, the analyst team may need to iteratively refine the results and engage with SMEs multiple times. Because of the iterative nature of this task and the potential for the system ranking results to be classified, most SME engagement can take place using emailed questionnaires and potentially informal follow-up email or phone discussions.

In addition to revising the CMTA results, this subphase may also provide insights into whether the CMTA methodology itself needs revising. That is, if the CMTA methodology does not identify a system that SMEs deem to be critical, or alternatively identifies a critical system that SMEs believe is not critical, the analysis team should understand why. If the mission thread is found to be correct, the CMTA methodology itself may need revising to. Feedback will improve the process.

The iterative and potentially ad hoc structure of this subphase would make it difficult for the analyst team to hold one working meeting, as proposed in previous subphases, to revise the CMTA results. Thus, we suggest that the final analyst team activities take place more informally, with the analyst team leader ushering the process. The briefing to leadership for their critical review should be implemented as deemed appropriate by the analyst team. These activities, as well as preparation for them (collation and review of notes and questionnaires) can be targeted to be completed within a week.

Conducting SME Engagements for Final Critical Review

For the second critical review of the CMTA, we suggest engaging both internal and external SMEs through emailed questionnaires and informal follow-up email discussions. If particular SMEs identify major issues in the initial questionnaire, however, the facilitator/interviewer might find it useful to hold follow-up phone interviews with a few them.

So as not to burden SMEs with unnecessary details, we suggest that the facilitator/interviewer only provide for review the final system rankings and the justification for this ranking (i.e., criticality criteria ratings for systems and the process used to translate these ratings into system rankings). Open-ended questions could be directed at these results. Further considerations for constructing this questionnaire are provided in Appendix A.

Follow-up interviews, then, could probe as deemed necessary and offer the revised mission thread for review as a supplement. As with previous SME interviews, we suggest that in addition to the interviewer and note-taker, a subset of the analyst team with relevant knowledge listen in.

Revising and Finalizing the Mission Thread and System Rankings

Upon completing the interviews and questionnaires, the note-taker should collate notes and, as with previous subphases, develop a summary to be sent to members of the analyst team. Based on the feedback provided by SMEs, the team leader can choose appropriate team member(s) to take the lead on revising the mission thread (noting that different team members may be appropriate for each). If any remaining issues arise (e.g., there is still confusion about a small branch of the mission thread), we suggest the facilitator/interviewer informally reach out to SMEs as necessary. Any disagreements (between SMEs or analyst team members) or uncertainties might be settled by the team leader and should be noted in the final results.

Time-Saving Variations

A number of factors may require the analyst team to seek out time-saving variations to the proposed analysis plan presented in the previous section. Here we describe a few adjustments to the analysis plan that may reduce the time required to implement the CMTA process but may also reduce the quality of the analysis.

First, information being elicited by phone interviews may be collected using email questionnaires instead. The analyst team may choose, for instance, to only interview two or three of the most relevant SMEs to inform the mission thread, sending the rest an email questionnaire.

If more than one focus group is required because SME numbers are large, another strategy to save time would be to hire a second facilitator and note-taker and conduct the focus groups simultaneously rather than serially. The analyst team members could split their time between the two focus groups.

Finally, a variation to the proposed analysis plan could also reduce the CMTA timeline. The analyst team could plan for two SME engagement activities instead of three. We currently propose that SMEs be engaged first to inform the mission thread, then to review the mission thread and finally to review the system ranking. An analysis plan could be constructed in which the analyst team forgoes the first external SME engagement, using only the analyst team knowledge and internal SMEs to construct the initial mission thread.

Of course, all of these time-saving variations may decrease the analyst team's confidence in the final results. If too many variations are adopted, there is a possibility that the analyst team may not be able to converge on a set of results, essentially resulting in failure of the overall objective. Thus, we recommend that time-saving variations be used sparingly and only as needed.

Performing Post-Analysis Activities

Once the CMTA is complete, the analyst team should formally document any lessons learned during the analysis, including those related to the preparation or the implementation of the analysis, as well as submissions of SME engagement materials developed and used. Chapter 5 offers further details on this documentation.

In the longer term, the final CMTA results may need to be reexamined periodically. The CONOPS of missions and design of systems under which operational missions must be considered all may change in the future. These factors may result in changes to the mission thread that introduce new systems or change the criticality of existing systems. The prioritization of systems for further cybersecurity assessments may therefore need to be adjusted. A natural point in which to do this reexamination might be once the CMTA has been completed for all missions. At that time, any missions with CONOPS changes or major system modifications could be candidates for reanalysis.

5. Adopting CMTA Process Efficiencies

We estimate that implementation of the CMTA process, as proposed in this report, may require eight weeks per mission but could take much longer if the planning phases (phases one and two) encounter issues or the mission is complex. In this chapter, we discuss efficiency strategies that could help the CMTA process owner and analyst team to improve the CMTA timeline within a specific mission, as well as across multiple missions.

Documenting, Collecting, and Leveraging Lessons Learned

The documentation of lessons learned is important not only to the efficiency with which CMTA is implemented, but also to its overall success. The analyst team should formally document lessons learned and, for at least for the first few CMTAs performed, this documentation should be a required deliverable when an executing organization submits CMTA results. These lessons learned could include the following:

- Lessons learned related to building the mission thread and conducting the system ranking. Agendas or strategies used during analyst team working meetings to meet the CMTA objectives may be included.
- Any issues with, or successful strategies used in, the analyst team's analysis plan, interview and focus group protocols, and questionnaires. The actual analysis plan, protocols, and questionnaires used can also be included.
- Lessons learned during the preparatory phases of the CMTA process (e.g., selecting and recruiting SMEs, collecting relevant documentation, analyst team qualifications and training). Emails sent to SME organizations or program offices may be provided as examples.

After receiving lessons-learned documentation from several missions, the CMTA process owner could summarize the findings. These summaries, as well as example emails, protocols, questionnaires, and even exemplar mission threads, could be made available to executing organizations before their implementation of CMTA. As the CMTA process owner collects additional lessons learned, the documentation should be routinely updated.

Referring to generalized lessons learned and successful analysis plans should improve the analyst team's timeline for completing the entire CMTA process. It will likely reduce the number of mistakes and retakes that occur during the implementation of CMTA. Additionally, the analyst team may be able to improve the timeline of its SME recruitment and analysis planning process by adapting existing protocols, questionnaires, SME recruitment emails, SME engagement handouts, and so on. Many of these documents should change only in topical focus. For instance, a question in an existing interview protocol that asks about how a specific function is performed may only need to change the name of the function. The question wording will likely not change.

Developing Mission Thread Templates

In addition to summarizing lessons learned, the CMTA process owner can accelerate the execution of future CMTAs by iteratively developing a set of mission thread templates that can be used by executing organizations. A number of commonalities exist across missions such that a generic mission structure, or template, may be used to begin the development of a mission thread. If the CMTA process owner develops and houses a repository for such templates, they can be made available to future executing organizations and likely improve the timeline for conducting the analysis (phase three). The templates can also be used to assist the analyst team when determining the gaps in expertise, as discussed in Chapter 2. That is, templates may inform the expertise needed to properly conduct the CMTA. These templates may further guide the protocols for the first SME engagements that inform the mission thread. In some instances, the interviewer may even find value in providing a specific template to the SMEs or giving them an overview of the mission. The interviewer could then ask the SME to focus the discussion about one or more modules in the template. Finally, the template would be very useful during the first analyst team working meeting to guide the development of the initial mission thread. However, while templates can be very helpful to inform the mission thread, they should also be used with caution. The analyst team or SMEs may be less likely to search for other mission thread branches, activities, and systems when provided with a template. Effort should be made to ensure that alternatives to the template are explored.

Designating Dedicated Analyst Teams or an Analyst Team Trainer

Given the learning curve needed to successfully execute a CMTA, the CMTA process owner and executing organization may decide to use the same analyst team to perform the analysis for a number of missions. While each member of an analyst team needs to have some relevant mission or system expertise, there may be a number of missions for which a dedicated analyst team could be assembled with appropriate expertise across missions. Designating such a dedicated analyst team would require advanced planning by the CMTA process owner and executing organization to identify where one analyst team could be used for multiple missions. Any lessons learned by this team in the first CMTA could create efficiencies for later CMTAs. Additionally, the team would gain familiarity with working with one another, which could also lead to efficiencies.

For certain missions, new analyst teams will undoubtedly need to be assembled. When any new analyst team is assembled, whether to perform a CMTA for one or many missions, the team members may benefit from training in the CMTA process. Designating someone to be an analyst team trainer, either within the CMTA process owner organization or the executing organization, could create efficiencies by allowing for better communication of CMTA process guidance and lessons learned.

Managing the Concurrency of CMTAs

CMTA analyses currently need to be performed for roughly 40 missions (Miller, Scarano, and Tashji, 2017). Even assuming an accelerated schedule of six weeks per mission, analyzing all missions would require nearly five years. Five years is too long to wait for addressing cyber deficiencies. Additionally, by the time all analyses would be completed, many of the CONOPS for these missions could change and require reanalysis. However, the CMTA process owner should be able to employ a few different management strategies to ameliorate such a situation. First, the CMTA process owner could assign CMTA analyses to be performed concurrently for multiple missions. These concurrent CMTAs could be performed by the same, or more than one, executing organization, but would likely need to have offset starting times to ensure that the CMTA process owner would be available when the phase of each process warrants.

Table 5.1 illustrates how this type of concurrency could be implemented. We assume that the CMTA process owner's schedule only allows for one major interaction with an executing organization at a time. Indeed, the CMTA process owner is likely to have other responsibilities beyond directing CMTAs. Table 5.1 shows how three executing organizations can concurrently perform CMTAs on three different missions, but more or fewer missions may be performed concurrently in a similar manner. Each executing organization is represented by a different color in the table, with the CMTA process owner's interactions with each organization color-coded accordingly. The CMTA process owner would stagger the selection of executing organizations and focus efforts on securing SME buy-in for each CMTA separately. By the time these interactions for the three CMTAs are complete, the first executing organization should have completed its initial mission thread. Thus, the CMTA process owner can shift to the role of critical reviewer in its relationship with the first executing organization. Critical review activities would then commence until the final of the three executing organizations had completed the CMTA, at which point, the CMTA process owner could begin the process again for three new missions.

Table 5.1. A Visualization of Concurrent CMTA Processes for Three Missions

CMTA Owner	Select executing org	Secure SME buy-in	Select executing org	Secure SME buy-in	Select executing org	Secure SME buy-in	Review of mission thread	Review of mission thread	Review of CMTA results	Review of mission thread	Review of CMTA results	Review of CMTA results
Executing Org 1		Establish roles and analysis inputs		Plan the analysis process	Conduct the analysis							
Executing Org 2				Establish roles and analysis inputs		Plan the analysis process	Conduct the analysis					
Executing Org 3						Establish roles and analysis inputs		Plan the analysis process	Conduct the analysis			

35

The strategy presented in Table 5.1 is merely an example of how the CMTA process owner could assign more than one mission to be analyzed concurrently. There are likely numerous variations on this example. However, given the number of missions that must be analyzed and the time constraints with which to do so, some kind of concurrency is needed and seems both possible and practical.

Managing the Order of CMTAs

One final approach the CMTA process owner could undertake for improving the overall CMTA timeline could be to strategically select the order in which missions are analyzed. For example, similar missions (whether that similarity exists in the activities undertaken or the weapon systems used) could be completed concurrently. In this case, the SMEs for such missions may overlap and therefore securing their buy-in for multiple missions could occur just once. On the other hand, the CMTA process owner may choose to separate similar missions over time, allowing lessons learned from one to be documented and then later made available to be leveraged for another. Templates could then be developed in the early CMTAs, allowing future CMTAs to achieve significantly shorter timelines.

6. Final Thoughts and Next Steps

In this implementation guide, we build on our companion methodology report by providing guidance for how to implement CMTA with the aim of executing the methodology as efficiently as possible while maintaining efficacy and providing results that credibly support decisionmaking. We draw on lessons learned from pilot applications of the CMTA, analogous efforts in the U.S. Air Force, and a survey of the relevant social science literature. Our guidance also takes into consideration that the CMTA process will be subject to a variety of real-world constraints—short overall timelines, limited SME availability, human error and bias—and strives to balance best practices and practical constraints to offer options that allow the most accurate information collection possible.

We reiterate that the process for implementing a CMTA as outlined in this report is an initial proposal. As further experience is gained, we fully expect that the process of doing CMTAs will improve and some of the details we propose in this report will be superseded. In that light, one final recommendation we stress for implementation of CMTA is that the proposed process, including the roles and responsibilities of CMTA stakeholders and the proposed analysis plan, be periodically revisited and revised.

We conclude this implementation guide by reiterating a few important points to keep in mind when planning and executing the CMTA process. The first two points are likely the most critical to efficiently and effectively implementing the CMTA process, but all points below should be considered if the effort is to be truly a success.

- *Planning is crucial.* To efficiently and effectively implement the CMTA process, the analyst team should develop and execute a detailed plan. The number of stakeholders involved and desire for a swift timeline require a substantial coordination effort. Without proper planning, the CMTA timeline could be significantly extended and the results of the analysis could be inadequate.
- *Remember the ultimate goal of CMTA.* Throughout the entire analysis, we stress the need for the analyst team to keep in mind the ultimate CMTA goal—producing a list of systems for further cyber assessments. The purpose is triage: It is vital that any mission-critical system appear highly ranked; it is okay if some noncritical systems appear highly ranked. Using this goal as a guiding principle for SME engagements and analyst team activities ensures that SME and analyst discussions do not become unnecessarily detailed and CMTA results remain within scope. As a result, the execution of the analysis is more likely to remain on schedule and achieve the desired level of efficiency.
- *Tailoring the process is necessary.* There is no one-size-fits-all model for implementing CMTA. The process will differ based on the complexity of the mission being analyzed, the classification level, the desired timeline, the available resources, and the level of expertise and availability of involved personnel. Therefore, while this implementation guide provides commonsense recommendations on how to plan and execute CMTA

under most circumstances, every CMTA exercise will present its own set of unique circumstances and therefore requires some degree of tailoring to successfully execute.

- *Periodic critical reviews on CMTA results by all CMTA stakeholders are important.* The CMTA exercise should be seen as a collaborative effort. The analyst team should both incorporate inputs from CMTA stakeholders and, importantly, elicit their feedback on the analytic products. Critical review will not only help to ensure CMTA results are accurate, but also foster stakeholder buy-in and instill credibility in the process. Ultimately, decisionmakers will have confidence in the results if the personnel involved are the best available and the process is transparent and reasonable.

- *Incorporate learning from prior CMTAs.* As CMTAs are performed for more missions, the CMTA process owner should develop a repository for lessons learned, sample CMTA materials (e.g., SME questionnaires), and mission thread templates. Analyst teams could make heavy use of such documents throughout the CMTA process.

- *CMTAs for multiple missions will likely need to be coordinated.* Given the number of missions needing analysis, a serial application of CMTAs may lead to a long overall time frame. Many of the CONOPS for missions could change in that time, requiring reanalysis. The CMTA process owner likely needs to assign multiple CMTAs to be performed concurrently. Proper management of this CMTA concurrency (e.g., ordering of missions) is crucial.

Appendix A. Further Considerations for Conducting SME Elicitations

This appendix serves as a reference for carrying out SME elicitations as part of CMTA. It covers specific recommendations as well as general information regarding conducting the SME interviews, focus groups, and questionnaires. Additionally, we provide sections on mitigating potential bias and process losses during the SME engagements.

Conducting Exploratory Interviews

General Guidance

As discussed in Chapter 3, exploratory interviews of SMEs are the preferred method for eliciting information to shape the initial mission thread. This interviewing style generally includes three question formats (Harrell and Bradley, 2009):

- *Descriptive* questions ask respondents to describe a topic of interest and may provide insights or suggest areas for further query that may not have been previously considered. Descriptive questions result in a narrative, and they should only be asked if the interviewer wants the respondent to take the time to answer with a narrative, which might be lengthy. They are process or "how" questions. For example, "How would you carry out an aerial refueling mission?"
- *Structural* questions help the interviewer to query about relationships between things and to categorize groups of like things or like processes. When asking these questions, it is important to explain and provide context and even examples so that respondents realize that the interviewer is attempting to develop a list. For example, "What information systems are connected to this system?"
- *Contrast* questions help differentiate between items on a list that the researcher has already obtained. For example, "Which of these actions is performed first?"

In addition, the interviewer may also need to use probing, follow-up questions when initial responses from SMEs do not provide enough detail, whether because they lack clarity or completeness. The following is a list of sample probes (derived from Harrell and Bradley, 2009) that an interviewer may employ in a CMTA context:

- For clarity/specificity
  - "Can you be more specific about the mission task required to complete that mission?"
  - "Can you tell me more about that mission task?"
  - "What is your best estimate of the number of systems connected to that one?"
- For completeness
  - "Are there any other mission tasks that need to be carried out for this mission?"
  - "Can you say more about that mission task?"

39

In addition, the interviewer can repeat the question, echo the SME's response, or pause to wait for the SME to provide more detail. The interviewer should understand when an answer is sufficient and thus discontinue probing.

CMTA-Specific Guidance

The SME interviews to inform the mission thread may take one of two forms: unstructured if the mission thread is relatively unknown to the analyst team, or semi-structured if the analyst team has reasonable knowledge of specific sections of the mission thread.

If the analyst team lacks knowledge or confidence on major portions of the mission thread, the protocol could follow an unstructured approach, using mostly descriptive questions. SMEs should receive little information before the engagement so as not to be primed to answer a certain way. A scoping statement about the mission area and the concepts of operations may suffice. One protocol for unstructured interviews that may perform well in the CMTA setting is that of a funnel design (Morgan et al., 2002): Begin with very general questions and then use follow-up probes having increasing specificity.[1] Questions for operators would likely begin with phrasing such as, "Tell me how mission X is performed," or "Take me through each step that needs to be accomplished in this mission." As the operator names mission tasks or functions, the interviewer would slowly probe deeper to obtain information about branches of the mission thread mentioned. For example, "You said that you would perform function X. Can you tell me how you would perform that?" If the operator names subfunctions, the interviewer may probe again, saying, "Can you tell me the activities that go into performing that subfunction?" Next, once the interviewer has probed as deep as necessary into a mission function, questions may shift to identifying systems: "You named activity X. What systems would you use to do that activity?" An important question to include in any protocol that elicits the mission thread is to identify potential workarounds. Probing questions in this instance may be, "If something happens and you can no longer perform the activity the way you described, is there another way to perform it? Are there other systems you could use?"

Interviews with a systems SME may take a slightly different approach to the funnel design. An interviewer may begin by querying, "Tell me all of the systems that are used as a part of this mission." As systems are named, the interviewer may probe, "How is this system used?" or "In what types of activities or tasks is this system used?" Follow-up questions may ensure there are no gaps in the information being elicited: "Can you think of any other ways this system is used?" Questions about workarounds for these SMEs may focus on the systems. For example, "What if this system was for some reason not available to be used in the task you described. Is there another system that could be used?" An appropriate follow-up question could then be, "If the

---

[1] If the analyst team engages SMEs using questionnaires, the questions could follow a similar format to that suggested for an interview.

mission activities were performed using workaround activity X, what other systems would be used?"

Importantly, questions posed by the interviewer should not inject new ideas into the interview and instead use wording and concepts introduced by the respondent. In this way, the interviewer elicits a clear mental model (Morgan et al., 2002) of how the SME thinks about that mission and the systems that support it and does not prime the SME with information previously understood by the analyst team. This type of unstructured questioning can be quite time-consuming.

One means of reducing the time commitment of both the analyst team and SMEs is to conduct semi-structured interviews using structured questioning, as an alternative to the unstructured approach described above. If the analyst team is relatively confident about major portions of the mission thread and only lacks knowledge in specific functions or thread branches, interviews can focus directly on those areas.

In this case, the interviewer could provide respondents with information before the interview that includes a scoping statement of the mission, a brief overview of the major mission functions as the analyst team understands them, and a statement about the functional areas (or systems in the case of a systems SME) to be covered during the interview. The interviewer's questioning would still be exploratory in nature (and mirror those provided earlier in this section), but instead direct the respondent to explain activities within a specific function. For example, questions would likely begin, "Tell me how function X is performed," or "Can you explain what happens next in this mission after function Y has been completed?" The interviewer would still probe as deep into the selected mission thread branch as necessary and ask about potential workarounds. Questions for systems SMEs would ask about specific systems identified by the interviewer (instead of leaving the flow of the interview up to the respondent).

As with all forms of SME elicitations—interviews, focus groups, and questionnaires—we recommend that the interview protocol for informing the initial mission thread be developed taking into consideration biases that could occur in questioning and responses (as discussed later in this appendix) and then pilot-tested. According to cognitive psychologists, pilot testing can be done by

- conducting think-aloud interviews, in which respondents read or are asked a question from the interview script or questionnaire under examination and then told to think aloud about the thoughts they are having as they try to absorb and answer the question (Fowler, 1995; Morgan et al., 2002)
- having respondents answer the question and then asking a series of questions that paraphrase their understanding of the question or whether there was anything confusing about it (Fowler, 1995).

Conducting Focus Groups

General Guidance

As discussed in Chapter 3, we propose that the external SME elicitation to review the initial mission thread take place as a focus group. As with interviews, developing a protocol is a vital step in maximizing the quality of information obtained from focus groups. Planning and prioritizing the questions helps to manage time more effectively and to avoid group process losses (as discussed later in this appendix). Descriptive and structural questions are both used in focus groups. Additional question types that may be used by a facilitator include the following:

- *Background* or *icebreaker* questions start off the discussion and are meant to get all participants comfortable talking. Such questions can also serve the purpose of obtaining important information about the SMEs, such as their past experience.
- *Anonymous* questions may be used when a subject matter is sensitive or controversial. The facilitator asks SMEs to write their answers on index cards and collects them, either for later analysis or to fuel the conversation without attributed responses to individual participants.
- *Kitchen sink* questions, which generally come toward the end, permit SMEs to discuss issues of importance to them that have not come up during the discussion.
- *Big-picture* questions usually come at or near the end of the focus group and can be helpful in uncovering themes and issues not previously considered (Harrell and Bradley, 2009).

While many of the probes used for interviewing are also appropriate to use during a focus group, probes specific to focus groups can be used to keep the conversation moving on topic, take control away from a dominant person, or draw out some of the quieter participants. Brainstorming techniques are also useful during focus groups. In terms of the quantity of ideas, the most effective way to brainstorm is for members of a group to generate ideas individually with no group interaction. The ideas are then collected and the redundant ones are eliminated. This approach eliminates production blocking, in which members' ideas are suppressed when listening to other members talk. Subsequently, groups might discuss the ideas in an evaluation phase and add additional ideas as they come up (Straus, 2017). Another brainstorming technique is *brainwriting*, where participants write down ideas rather than speak them aloud and exchange the written ideas, using them to stimulate new ones. Some studies have found that brainwriting groups produce more ideas than do verbal brainstorming groups (Michinov, 2012).

In addition to preparing and executing the questioning, the facilitator of a focus group must act as a moderator. The facilitator is often called on to mitigate the influence of certain individuals who might have strong influence over the group interaction. Strong influence may occur if someone has a high rank or even if they are voluble or enthusiastic. If other participants feel intimidated or unknowledgeable relative to such an individual, dynamic conversation may cease. The facilitator should ensure that all SMEs are heard, both by encouraging others to speak as well as suggesting that dominating SMEs do not completely take over the conversation. A facilitator may also need to separate close colleagues prior to the start of the group in order to avoid side conversations or so that other participants do not feel excluded or outnumbered. The facilitator should further be ready for participants who have no real desire to participate productively in the group interaction; they may appear hostile or threatening and can damage a group's interaction. Sometimes a skilled facilitator can convert this person with humor or understanding; however, if this is not possible, the facilitator may need to ask the person to leave. Often a moderator will use a five-minute break to privately dismiss a problem individual from the group (Harrell and Bradley, 2009).

CMTA-Specific Guidance

In the case of the SME focus group to review the initial mission thread, discussions about each branch of the mission thread should follow a similar, methodical format. After the relevant mission thread branch has been projected overhead for the SMEs, the facilitator can direct the SMEs to take five minutes to jot down their initial thoughts about the branch—what's missing, wrong, or confusing. As previously discussed, asking group members to write down their thoughts before engaging in a discussion can overcome a few group dynamic issues that are commonly found during group deliberation processes (Straus, Parker, and Bruce, 2011). First, the activity gives SMEs an opportunity to react to the mission thread without being primed by others' ideas. Second, launching directly into discussion may lead some group members to focus their attention on processing others' thoughts, limiting their time to generate thoughts of their own.

Next, the facilitator could open the floor for discussion using a phrase such as, "Can one person begin by telling everyone what they noted about this branch of the mission thread?" To engage other SMEs in the discussion, the facilitator could follow up with another question such as, "Did anyone else have a similar thing noted?" And to elicit any disagreement, the facilitator could ask, "Does anyone disagree with these thoughts? Why?" The facilitator might ensure that everyone has a chance to speak by specifically calling out SMEs who have not volunteered their thoughts. For instance, "We haven't heard from you. Do you agree with what everyone else is saying? Did you take notes on any points that have not been discussed yet?" If the group is not volunteering their thoughts, the facilitator can methodically touch on each activity and system in the mission branch by saying, "No one has brought up how activity X or the systems used for activity X are represented. Does everyone agree that they are represented correctly?"

The facilitator could close each group discussion about a function with one final set of open-ended questions: "Is there anything else that we haven't discussed about this branch that we should be covering? Are there any other systems that can be used during this function? Are there any other activities that we haven't discussed?"

Developing Questionnaires

General Guidance

When developing a questionnaire, the overall structure must be designed first. It should begin with instructions and a description of who should fill out the questionnaire, and each section should be given an appropriate heading. Providing the contact information of the facilitator/ interviewer is useful in case respondents have questions. The questionnaire should group questions by topic, with any particularly interesting questions included first to help motivate respondents to complete it. Generally, it is a good idea to put any demographic questions at the end, as these tend to be the least interesting. The length and the amount of time required to complete the questionnaire should also be considered during its design (Lazar, Feng, and Hochheiser, 2010).

Respondents need to be motivated to fill out the questionnaire. For example, an introductory letter letting people know of their selection by their leadership for their expertise can be helpful. The letter should say who is sponsoring the study, why the study is important, and what the expected time frame is. It should also establish some authority or credibility. If a respected individual, such as a senior leader in the organization, introduces the questionnaire, this can help establish authority. Finally, it is advisable to make the questionnaire easy to return (Lazar, Feng, and Hochheiser, 2010).

CMTA-Specific Guidance

For the final critical review of the CMTA results, we recommend that the questionnaire begin with questions about the system ranking. Questions could ask, "Do you think the results of the system ranking are logical? Is there anything that surprises you? Why? Are there any systems completely missing from the list?" If any SMEs answer that they believe the ordering of the ranking is incorrect, they could be directed to the ratings that were assigned for each criticality criterion for the systems. SMEs could be asked to review this information and provide comments. If, instead, any SMEs believe that a system is missing from the list altogether, they could be directed to the mission thread. The questionnaire could query about where that system would be placed within the mission thread. For all questions, SMEs can be probed to explain why something seems wrong and how it could be fixed. That is, the questionnaire should not only stress the importance of the SMEs pointing out issues with the CMTA results, but also providing their reasoning.

Mitigating Potential Bias

No individual is immune to biases. As humans, our information processing and decisionmaking is influenced by bias. Recognition of this bias is important to successfully implementing a CMTA. The facilitator/interviewer, as well as the entire analyst team, should consider and try to ameliorate the potential biases that can arise during SME elicitation. Biases may be generally categorized as *motivational* or *cognitive*. Motivational biases tend to be driven by our human needs, such as the need for approval, whereas cognitive biases are driven by constraints in our ability to process information (Meyer and Booker, 2001). Cognitive biases are commonly referred to as heuristics (Hastie and Dawes, 2010). Both types of bias may affect SMEs. In this section, we introduce common biases that may arise in the CMTA setting as well as methods the facilitator/interviewer may use to reduce them.

Motivational Bias

Common motivational biases[2] that may impact CMTA SME elicitations include those related to social pressures on SMEs, including from interviewers, other elicitation participants, and even from people who are not present. First, SMEs may adjust how they answer a question because of concerns over the acceptability of their responses by the interviewer. This bias may arise from the interviewer's framing of the question (e.g., asking a leading question), from the interviewer's verbal and nonverbal responses to a SME's previous answers, or from a SME's perception of what the interviewer thinks to be a "correct" answer. To mitigate this type of bias, an interviewer should use care when developing questions, avoid leading questions (which would assure SMEs of the interviewer's neutrality), make clear that there are no right or wrong answers, and maintain neutral responses to the SME's answers.

Furthermore, *groupthink* is another form of social pressure in which the presence of other SMEs in the room causes someone to modify their responses or silently acquiesce to what they believe is acceptable to the group. A facilitator can help to avoid this social pressure through a number of different actions, including warning focus group participants about the bias, asking for the views of leaders or high-ranking individuals last, asking all focus group members to show up in civilian clothes, and asking participants to write down their thoughts before group discussion begins.

Finally, social pressure may even come from individuals who are not present. An individual may change their answers to questions based on the perceived reaction of others, such as a supervisor. For example, SMEs may be reluctant to state that they use systems that are not those recommended for a certain mission activity because they believe the recommended system is inadequate or inefficient. However, this type of information is critical to developing an accurate mission thread. The facilitator/interviewer can mitigate this form of bias by assuring SMEs that responses will not be attributed to anyone in particular.

One more motivational bias worthy of note is that which can also arise from the analyst team's interpretation of SME answers, based on the team's knowledge, training, and experience. This form of bias is of most concern when using questionnaires that do not allow for the opportunity to ask follow-up or clarifying questions. The best way to mitigate such bias is to

---

[2] Discussion of motivational bias in this section is derived from Meyer and Booker (2001).

properly word questions such that SMEs understand and answer the question as intended by the facilitator/interviewer. This can be managed through pilot testing and iterative refinement of questions, as discussed earlier in this appendix.

Cognitive Bias

A number of cognitive biases or heuristics are also likely to impact SME elicitations. Heuristics are essentially mental shortcuts and are used by individuals when they need to make quick judgments because it eases the cognitive load (Hastie and Dawes, 2010; Ayyub, 2001a; Galway, 2007; Kahneman, Slovic, and Tversky, 1982; Morgan and Henrion, 1990). Time and resources are generally limited. Therefore, people have developed simple processes to make complex decisions, and as expressed by Tversky and Kahneman (1974, p. 1124), they "are quite useful, but sometimes . . . lead to severe and systematic errors." Those errors are the concern when eliciting information from SMEs. However, understanding these heuristics and using strategies for mitigating them can greatly improve the elicitation and the reliability of its results.

Common heuristic processes[3] that may impact CMTA SME elicitations include *anchoring and adjusting, overconfidence,* and *primacy effects.* First, in uncertain situations, information sometimes even of trivial importance may form an "anchor" for individuals that serves as a starting point for estimation or decisionmaking. Individuals may then evaluate any new information that can influence their decision in light of this trivial information. They may "under adjust" their decision because of the original anchor. An example of how this *anchor and adjust* heuristic could manifest itself in the CMTA process is if a facilitator presents SMEs with an initial mission thread. SMEs may anchor on the initial thread and may therefore not explore as many alternative ways a mission could be completed. In this specific example, the heuristic could be avoided by not priming SMEs with any information the first time they are questioned about a mission thread. If information must be presented to SMEs before an elicitation, only that which is critical should be provided. Second, the facilitator/interviewer should be aware that SMEs are commonly overconfident in estimates or information they provide. That is, SMEs tend to underestimate the uncertainty surrounding a quantity or answer they provide. A good CMTA facilitator/interviewer can mitigate this overconfidence with additional probing questions, such as, "Are there other unlikely but possible ways this function could be performed?" or "Can you think of an argument for why the answer/explanation you provided would not be true?" One final relevant heuristic in the context of CMTA is that people tend to exhibit a *primacy effect* or weigh more heavily information considered early in a judgment process (Hastie and Dawes, 2010; Tversky and Kahneman, 1974; Chapman and Bornstein, 1996). Anchoring and adjusting is one form of a primacy effect, but the heuristic also applies more generally. A facilitator/interviewer should therefore be very careful about the order in which information is presented.

---

[3] Discussion of heuristics in this section is derived from Hastie and Dawes (2010).

While we provide mitigation strategies for specific motivation and cognitive biases, some more general strategies may also be applied that can ameliorate bias overall. Many of these strategies are discussed in the main body of the report. We summarize the most important ones here for emphasis and comprehensiveness.

First, following a systematic elicitation method can vastly mitigate bias. For example, a focus group facilitator who develops a protocol beforehand will have a chance to craft questions that do not prime or lead the SME. A systematic method provides the facilitator/interviewer with a plan. It also makes the elicitation more reproducible, easier to document, and more controllable (Morgan and Henrion, 1990; Ayyub, 2001b). Second, many researchers suggest that experts be "trained" before an elicitation (Ayyub, 2001a; Morgan and Henrion, 1990; Meyer and Booker, 2001). Training may involve teaching experts about potential biases they may encounter and providing detailed background materials about the subject matter in question (e.g., about CMTA). This strategy helps SMEs mitigate their own tendencies toward bias and be aware of potential biases of the facilitator/interviewer. Finally and importantly, the facilitator/interviewer may greatly benefit from pilot testing the protocol with at least one SME to ensure it is understandable and reasonable.

Mitigating Group Process Losses

Any aspect of a group interaction that can inhibit problem-solving is referred to as a group process loss (Straus, Parker, and Bruce, 2011). Group process losses can lead to less accurate information, time wasted, or overconfidence in gathered information. These process losses are commonly found to occur during focus group brainstorming sessions and often can override the benefits gained from a group interaction (Straus, Parker, and Bruce, 2011, Dalal et al., 2011). Common group process losses relevant to the CMTA context include the following:

- *Productivity losses.* Listening to others and waiting for a turn to speak can inhibit production of new ideas. As the group gets larger, this effect can be more pronounced.
- *Groupthink.* The desire for group solidarity leads group members to seek consensus and avoid identification and critical evaluation of alternatives.
- *Common knowledge effect.* Relevant information held by a minority of the group might not be introduced into the group discussion and, when mentioned, may be overlooked. Time pressure exacerbates this effect, and large groups with more than ten participants are more susceptible.
- *Confirmation bias.* Individuals tend to focus on information discussed in a group setting that supports their preconceived notions and not acknowledge information that contradicts it.
- *Interdependencies among process losses.* Processes can be mutually reinforcing, and the presence of one type of loss increases the likelihood that the group will experience other losses. When one type has been averted, the group is less prone to other types (Straus, Parker, and Bruce, 2011).

When conducting focus groups, process losses should be minimized to extract the highest-quality information possible. Process loss mitigation strategies include

- utilizing an effective facilitator who encourages open discussion and dissent
- striving for heterogeneity of group members' opinions and expertise
- restricting members from stating their preferences until all relevant information about the topic at hand has been shared
- requiring members to consider other and less likely alternatives and unexpected outcomes
- asking members to consider the uncertainty in the information being discussed
- presenting concepts all at once, rather than each concept sequentially (Straus, Parker, and Bruce, 2011).

Appendix B. CMTA Analyst Team Checklist

Phase One: Establish Roles and Analysis Inputs

1. Gather and Review Reference Documents

- ☐ Collect relevant DoDAF documents (i.e., OV-1, OV-6, SV-1, SV-6)
- ☐ Collect needed supplemental documents
    - ☐ Systems engineering artifacts that describe functional and data flows, interfaces, etc., as available from program offices
    - ☐ All relevant U.S. Air Force instructions and doctrines, as well as U.S. Air Force tactics, techniques, and procedures (TTPs)
    - ☐ Relevant "Dash-1s" and maintenance manuals
    - ☐ JCIDs artifacts, including capabilities-based assessments, initial capabilities documents (which could be used to identify mission-critical functions), and capability development documents for key performance parameters (KPPs) and key system attributes, all of which can be gathered from the associated operating MAJCOM
    - ☐ CONOPS from the associated operating MAJCOM, which describe how systems will be employed to execute various missions
    - ☐ Analysis of alternatives (AoAs) from the associated operating MAJCOM or program office, which may provide useful insight into the aspects of performance that led to the selection of the preferred system concept
    - ☐ Critical operations issues, which emerge from KPPs and are compiled by operational testers to evaluate whether a system will be effective for its mission requirements. These may be useful to identify critical functions in the system
    - ☐ Program protection plans, which are developed by the program offices and provide details of system protection, including critical program information, mission-critical functions performed by the system, and planned cybersecurity measures
- ☐ Review relevant documents to inform the types of SMEs needed
    - ☐ Produce a list of mission areas and systems for which quality, detailed information does not exist

2. Identify and Recruit SMEs

- ☐ Determine gaps in expertise
    - ☐ Conduct an inventory of the analyst team's current expertise and knowledge
    - ☐ Compare the inventory to expertise needed to conduct CMTA
    - ☐ Consider whether SMEs exist internal to the executing organization

- ☐ Identify relevant SME organizations
    - ☐ Operational community
        - ☐ Operational wings of major command mission-owners
        - ☐ Maintenance, support, and medical groups
    - ☐ Engineering and systems community
        - ☐ Relevant program offices and contractors
            - ☐ Lead system and subsystems engineers
            - ☐ System-security engineers
- ☐ Contact relevant organizations
    - ☐ Work with CMTA process owner to secure organization buy-in and recruit SMEs
    - ☐ Determine the identified SMEs' specific expertise, constraints, and time availability

Phase Two: Plan the Analysis Process

1. Build an Analysis Plan

- ☐ Consider situational factors, including internal knowledge, number and availability of SMEs, mission complexity, and desired timeline
- ☐ Choose the type of SME engagements: exploratory interviews, focus groups, or open-ended questionnaires
- ☐ Choose mode of SME engagements: email, phone calls, videoconference, or in-person
- ☐ Determine other analyst team activities
    - ☐ Planning and logistics
    - ☐ Analysis (i.e., build the mission thread and identify relevant systems for ranking, refine the mission thread and systems after critical review, conduct the system rankings, and refine the system rankings after critical review)
    - ☐ Internal and external SME engagements
    - ☐ Interactions with the CMTA process owner and the executing organization
    - ☐ Document lessons learned

2. Plan Logistics, Materials, and Protocols

- ☐ Schedule SME engagements
    - ☐ Survey SME availability
    - ☐ Collect SME contact information for phone interviews or emailed questionnaires
    - ☐ Choose dates and locations for all activities
    - ☐ Email meeting invitations to SMEs
    - ☐ Reserve conference rooms and ensure proper focus group resources are available (e.g., overhead projector)

- [ ] Schedule analyst team working meetings
  - [ ] Reserve conference rooms and resources as necessary
- [ ] Schedule briefings to the CMTA process owner and the executing organization
- [ ] Develop SME engagement materials

Phase Three: Conduct the Analysis

1. Develop Mission Thread

- [ ] Review relevant documentation and draw on in-house knowledge
- [ ] Elicit information from SMEs
  - [ ] Provide SMEs with introductory material before eliciting information, such as
    - Brief introduction to the concept of a mission thread and the objectives of CMTA
    - Objectives of the initial engagement activity
  - [ ] Perform SME engagement activity
  - [ ] Capture relevant information in notes
    - Review and clean the notes immediately after an interview while the information is still fresh
    - Have other team members review and edit to ensure all relevant information has been captured
  - [ ] Analyze findings on major themes, contradictory information, disagreements, and areas needing further clarification
- [ ] Sketch initial mission thread
  - [ ] Generate a breakdown of the mission into mission functions and discuss each function
  - [ ] Create a functional flow block diagram
  - [ ] Identify outstanding issues such as disagreements between team members or points where clarification is needed

2. Revise Mission Thread

- [ ] Request a critical review of the mission thread from both internal and external SMEs
  - [ ] Develop a detailed plan for SME engagement activity
    - [ ] An agenda
    - [ ] Materials to be provided before or during the focus group
    - [ ] Slides to be projected
    - [ ] Specific questions and probes to be used throughout the group session

- ☐ Send the mission thread to SMEs ahead of engagement activity and email additional materials, such as
    - ☐ A brief introduction to the concept of a mission thread and objectives of CMTA (again)
    - ☐ The objectives of the focus group session
    - ☐ An exemplar of a completed and vetted mission thread[1] so that SMEs can understand the level of detail and scope desired
    - ☐ Directions for SMEs to review the mission thread, to take notes on parts of the thread that might be incorrect, missing, or confusing, and to bring along to the session any relevant documentation
- ☐ Perform SME engagement activity
    - ☐ Provide SMEs with an agenda with time in the morning to review all of the emailed materials (i.e., the facilitator can introduce the CMTA process and the objectives of the group session and briefly walk SMEs through the initial mission thread in its entirety before inviting SME feedback)
    - ☐ Engage SMEs in discussion
- ☐ Capture relevant information in notes
    - ☐ Review and clean the notes immediately after an interview while the information is still fresh
    - ☐ Have other team members review and edit to ensure all relevant information has been captured
- ☐ Analyze findings on major themes, contradictory information, disagreements, and areas needing further clarification
- ☐ Engage internal SMEs
- ☐ Brief the CMTA process owner and executing organization leadership to elicit their feedback
- ☐ Revise mission thread
    - ☐ Review findings from SME engagements and leadership briefings
    - ☐ Update existing functional flow block diagram
    - ☐ Identify outstanding issues such as disagreements between team members or points where clarification is needed

3. Rank Systems

- ☐ Perform cut set analysis
- ☐ Determine criticality criteria (e.g., system dependencies, cyber separability) for each system
- ☐ Perform ranking based on criticality criteria

---

[1] This exemplar could be a mission thread completed for a previous CMTA or possibly a simple mission thread constructed solely for the purpose of this example—one that is small in scope and understandable to all SMEs.

4. *Review CMTA Results*

- ☐ Request a review of ranking from both internal and external SMEs
    - ☐ Send ranking to SMEs ahead of engagement activity
    - ☐ Perform SME engagement activity
    - ☐ Capture relevant information in notes
- ☐ Brief the CMTA process owner and executing organization leadership to elicit their feedback
- ☐ Iteratively revise criticality criteria and mission thread as necessary based on SME and leadership feedback

References

Air Force Materiel Command Office of Aerospace Studies, *High Performance Team (HPT) Facilitation Guidebook: A Methodology for Planning and Facilitating AoA Study Guidance and AoA Study Plan HPTs*, 2014.

Ayyub, Bilal M., *Elicitation of Expert Opinions for Uncertainty and Risks*, Boca Raton, Fla.: CRC Press, 2001a.

———, *A Practical Guide on Conducting Expert-Opinion Elicitation of Probabilities and Consequences for Corps Facilities*, January 2001b. As of August 25, 2017: http://www.iwr.usace.army.mil/Portals/70/docs/iwrreports/01-R-01.pdf

Babbie, Earl R., *The Practice of Social Research*, Belmont, Calif.: Thomson Wadsworth, 2007.

Chapman, Gretchen B., and Brian H. Bornstein, "The More You Ask For, the More You Get: Anchoring in Personal Injury Verdicts," *Applied Cognitive Psychology*, Vol. 10, No. 6, 1996, pp. 519–540.

Dalal, S., D. Khodyakov, R. Srinivasan, S. Straus, and J. Adams, "ExpertLens: A System for Eliciting Opinions from a Large Pool of Non-Collocated Experts with Diverse Knowledge," *Technological Forecasting and Social Change*, Vol. 78, No. 8, October 2011, pp. 1426–1444.

Department of Defense Chief Information Office, "DoDAF Viewpoints and Models," 2017. As of September 12, 2017: http://dodcio.defense.gov/Library/DoD-Architecture-Framework/dodaf20_viewpoints/

DoD CIO—*See* Department of Defense Chief Information Office.

Fowler, Floyd J., *Improving Survey Questions: Design and Evaluation*, Vol. 38, Thousand Oaks, Calif.: Sage Publications, 1995.

Galway, Lionel A., *Subjective Probability Distribution Elicitation in Cost Risk Analysis: A Review*, Santa Monica, Calif.: RAND Corporation, TR-410-AF, 2007. As of September 8, 2017: http://www.rand.org/pubs/technical_reports/TR410.html

Harrell, Margaret C., and Melissa A. Bradley, *Data Collection Methods: Semi-Structured Interviews and Focus Groups*, Santa Monica, Calif.: RAND Corporation, TR-718-USG, 2009. As of August 3, 2017: https://www.rand.org/pubs/technical_reports/TR718.html

Hastie, Reid, and Robyn M. Dawes, *Rational Choice in an Uncertain World: The Psychology of Judgment and Decision Making*, 2nd ed., Thousand Oaks, Calif.: Sage Publications, 2010.

Kahneman, Daniel, Paul Slovic, and Amos Tversky, eds., *Judgment Under Uncertainty: Heuristics and Biases*, Cambridge: Cambridge University Press, 1982.

Krueger, Richard A., and Mary Anne Casey, *Focus Groups: A Practical Guide for Applied Research*, Thousand Oaks, Calif.: Sage Publications, 2014.

Lazar, Jonathan, Jinjuan Heidi Feng, and Harry Hochheiser, *Research Methods in Human-Computer Interaction*, Chichester, UK: John Wiley & Sons, 2010.

Leonard, J., *Systems Engineering Fundamentals*, Fort Belvoir, Va.: Department of Defense Systems Management College, December 1999. As of September 12, 2017: http://www.dtic.mil/get-tr-doc/pdf?AD=ADA372635

Lynch, K., personal communication with the authors, March 20, 2017.

Meyer, M. A., and J. M. Booker, *Eliciting and Analyzing Expert Judgment: A Practical Guide*, American Statistical Society for Industrial and Applied Mathematics, 2001.

Michinov, N., "Is Electronic Brainstorming or Brainwriting the Best Way to Improve Creative Performance in Groups? An Overlooked Comparison of Two Idea-Generation Techniques," *Journal of Applied Sociology*, Vol. 42, No. S1, 2012, pp. E222–E243.

Miller, D. M., J. Scarano, and D. Tashji, "Identify and Prioritize Missions for Cyber Mission Thread Analysis," U.S Air Force Life Cycle Management Center, June 6, 2017.

MITRE, personal communication with the authors, April 13, 2017.

Morgan, D. L., *The Focus Group Guidebook*, Vol. 1, Thousand Oaks, Calif.: Sage Publications, 1997.

Morgan, M. G., B. Fischhoff, A. Bostrom, and C. J. Atman, *Risk Communication: A Mental Models Approach*, Cambridge: Cambridge University Press, 2002.

Morgan, M. Granger, and Max Henrion, *Uncertainty: A Guide to Dealing with Uncertainty in Quantitative Risk and Policy Analysis*, Cambridge: Cambridge University Press, 1990.

Paulus, P. B., and H. C. Yang, "Idea Generation in Groups: A Basis for Creativity in Organizations," *Organizational Behavior and Human Decision Processes*, Vol. 82, No. 1, May 2000, pp. 76–87.

Robson, Colin, *Real World Research: A Resource for Social Scientists and Practitioner-Researchers*, 2nd ed., Hoboken, N.J.: Blackwell, 2002.

Ryan, G. W., and H. R. Bernard, "Techniques to Identify Themes," *Field Methods*, Vol. 15, No. 1, February 2003, pp. 85–109.

Snyder, Don, Elizabeth Bodine-Baron, Dahlia Anne Goldfeld, Bernard Fox, Myron Hura, Mahyar A. Amouzegar, and Lauren Kendrick, *Cyber Mission Thread Analysis: A Prototype Framework for Assessing Impact to Missions from Cyber Attacks to Weapon Systems*, Santa Monica, Calif.: RAND Corporation, RR-3188/1-AF, 2022.

Straus, Susan G., personal communication with the authors, June 7, 2017.

Straus, Susan G., Andrew M. Parker, and James B. Bruce, "The Group Matters: A Review of Processes and Outcomes in Intelligence Analysis," *Group Dynamics-Theory Research and Practice*, Vol. 15, No. 2, 2011, pp. 128–146.

Tversky, Amos, and Daniel Kahneman, "Judgment Under Uncertainty: Heuristics and Biases," *Science*, Vol. 185, No. 4157, 1974, pp. 1124–1131.

Viola, Nicole, Sabrina Corpino, Marco Fioriti, and Fabrizio Stesina, "Functional Analysis in Systems Engineering: Methodology and Applications," in Boris Cogan, ed., *Systems Engineering—Practice and Theory*, London: IntechOpen, 2012. As of September 12, 2017: https://www.intechopen.com/books/systems-engineering-practice-and-theory/functional -analysis-in-systems-engineering-methodology-and-applications

Wainfan, Lynne, and Paul K. Davis, *Challenges in Virtual Collaboration: Videoconferencing, Audioconferencing, and Computer-Mediated Communications*, Santa Monica, Calif.: RAND Corporation, MG-273, 2004. As of August 15, 2017: https://www.rand.org/pubs/monographs/MG273.html